GOOD
HOUSEKEEPING

HOLIDAY COOKIES

100+ FUN AND FESTIVE TREATS

HEARST
HOME

CONTENTS

STRAWBERRY
PINWHEELS
page 104

There's no place like home for the holidays—but the *Good Housekeeping* Test Kitchen is a close second.

During the course of the year, our test kitchen team bakes around a thousand cookies and goes through more than 30 pounds of confectioners' sugar to make Royal Icing again and again. So you might think that by the time the holiday season rolls around, we're all a little cookied out. Nope! There's something truly magical about the stretch between Thanksgiving and New Year's: The sugar tastes a little sweeter, the cookies feel a little more fanciful and the recipes are just that much better.

So it's time we let you in on our secrets. Here, we're sharing more than 100 of our all-time favorite holiday cookie recipes. Each one has been tested for success in the Good Housekeeping Test Kitchen, so you can bake with confidence at home.

This festive collection will get you and your family (even the tiniest of chefs) creating new cookie baking traditions. There are familiar sweets (like Holiday Spritz Cookies, page 20), go-tos (like the Classic Sugar Cookie Dough, page 82), entirely new cookies (hello, Yuzu Crinkle Cookies, page 62) and even my family's favorite (Chocolate Chip Mandel Bread, page 44). Plus people around the world celebrate the winter holidays with their own traditional cookie and we've included those too (see Nan-e Berenji, page 48 and Nankhatai, page 30).

Besides dozens of tasty treats, we're also giving you a solid crash course on all things cookies: tips and techniques for decorating, a step-by-step guide to throwing the best-ever cookie swap party and genius ways to freeze and gift goodies—all so you can create sweet memories that last long after the last crumb is enjoyed.

Happy Baking,
Kate Merker
Chief Food Director

HOLIDAY SPRITZ COOKIES
page 20

GLAZED
ALMOND
CUTOUTS
page 40

CHAPTER 1

HOLIDAY COOKIE HOW-TOS

Oh what fun! In this holly-jolly guide you'll find our top secrets to hosting a perfect cookie swap, pro-level decorating skills and fail-safe shipping advice, so you can share the cookie love with everyone you know.

Decorating 101

With these recipes—and a complete step-by-step guide to icing and flooding—
you'll be confidently decorating cookies in no time at all.

ROYAL ICING

Active Time 5 minutes
Total Time 12 minutes
Makes 2 to 4 cups

  3 large egg whites
 ½ teaspoon cream of tartar
 16 ounces confectioners' sugar
     Gel food coloring, optional

1. Using an electric mixer, whisk egg whites and cream of tartar in a large bowl on medium-high speed until foamy, about 1 minute.

2. Reduce speed to low and gradually add sugar, beating until just incorporated. Increase speed to high and beat until medium-stiff glossy peaks form, 5 to 7 minutes.

3. To add color: Separate icing into bowls and tint different colors with gel food coloring, then transfer to separate piping bags fitted with fine tips.

MAKE AHEAD
Store Royal Icing in a bowl (with plastic pressed directly onto the surface) at room temperature for up to 2 days or in the refrigerator for up to 1 week. Bring to room temperature before using.

DECORATOR'S ICING

Active Time 5 minutes
Total Time 10 minutes
Makes 3 cups

- 16   ounces confectioners' sugar
- 3   tablespoons meringue powder
- ⅓   cup warm water
  Gel food coloring, optional

1. Using an electric mixer, beat confectioners' sugar, meringue powder and warm water in a large bowl on medium speed until blended and mixture is very stiff, about 5 minutes.

2. Tint icing with food coloring as desired; press plastic wrap directly onto surface to prevent it from drying out.

3. When ready to decorate, use a small spatula or piping bags fitted with small writing tips to ice cookies.

Ice Like a Pro

Master the art of flooding in just a few easy steps.

Mix up a batch of Royal Icing (left) or Decorator's Icing (above). Tint with gel food coloring if desired. Thin out half with a few drops of water until it looks like honey, then pop both the thick and thin icings into two separate piping bags.

1. OUTLINE
Use the thick icing to pipe a border around your cookie and let set (this keeps the sweet stuff from escaping).

2. FLOOD
Fill in the outline with the thin icing, then use a toothpick to quickly drag it to the edges and join the outline.

3. SPRINKLE
Add sanding sugar or nonpareils while the icing is still slightly wet, so they stick. Then let set.

ALTERNATE ICING
Decorator's Icing is made with meringue powder (a baking substitute created from dried egg whites, available at specialty stores or online) instead of raw eggs, making it safe option for those who are pregnant.

Host the Perfect Cookie Swap

Get ready to sprinkle some joy and swap some treats with our essential guide.

Your Cookie Swap Countdown

You don't have to be an experienced baker to host a cookie exchange. Get the party started with our step-by-step tips for success as the host with the most.

3 TO 4 WEEKS BEFORE

Invite family and friends
The most magical time of the year is also the busiest one, so send out those invites well in advance. Each guest should bring 6 to 12 cookies per guest attending (so for a party of five, each person would bring 30 to 60 cookies). Ask attendees for the name of their cookie when they RSVP so you can head off any duplicates. A thoughtful extra: Ask each guest to bake an extra dozen, and create a tray to bring to a local shelter, hospital, retirement home or family in need. (See page 11 for a couple charities to support this giving season.)

Choose your own cookie
Select a recipe you know and love — and one that you can easily make multiple batches of. Opt for a sturdy cookie that won't break or crumble during the swap.

1 TO 3 DAYS BEFORE

Make your cookies
Don't wait until the last minute. Prep any parts of your recipe that can be made in advance to avoid a time crunch, like making the cookie dough and stashing it in the fridge a day or two before baking.

Prep no-cook appetizers
Put together beautiful cheese and charcuterie boards instead of fussing over hot hors d'oeuvres. Include an assortment of cured meats, cheeses, olives, crackers, grapes, spiced nuts and spreads.

Set up a self-serve cocktail bar
Forget stocking a bar cart with endless options. Decide on one or two seasonal picks to make ahead then let guests serve themselves from pitchers or punch bowls.

2 WEEKS BEFORE

Gather the recipes
Send out a recipe card template for each guest to fill out pre-party, then print copies for everyone to take home. Or create a digital cookbook: Start a shared document with recipe card templates, then share the link and have everyone fill in their cookie's details.

Plan for packaging
Start gathering tins, plastic tubs, mason jars or small gift boxes to repurpose as cookie carriers — ask your guests to pitch in too and cut down on costs. Or buy reusable airtight containers for everyone to design with markers, paint pens, stickers or other quick, no-fuss decorations during the party.

Set your menu
Sure the cookies are the stars, but every swap party needs drinks and savory snacks to offset all that sweetness (see page 12 for some of our favorites).

THE BIG DAY

Label the cookies
Encourage guests to dig in by setting out each cookie's recipe card next to each platter. This way guests can easily identify the treat and who made it, plus any potential allergens.

Don't forget to relax
You earned it! Kick back, have fun and enjoy the company — and the cookies!

Gather and Give Back

Give your cookie swap a charitable twist with some bonus cookies and crafts — for a good cause. These organizations help those in need in the holiday season.

COOKIES FOR KIDS' CANCER

What started as a 96,000-cookie bake-athon has since led to a movement of more than 15,000 bake sales across all 50 states and 24 countries. The results: More than $20 million has been raised for pediatric cancer research, and dozens of new treatments have been funded in the process. Host your own fundraiser or cookie swap with a feel-good focus — the organization has lots of resources on its site (cookiesforkidscancer.org) to help raise even more money.

THE ANGEL CARD PROJECT

Volunteer to send holiday cards to people who need a little extra cheer this year. This organization shares a list of names and addresses with everyone who signs up, so all you have to do is fill out a card and an envelope, add a stamp, and send. But for a more festive alternative, you can host a card-crafting party instead! Set out card stock, envelopes, extra magazines and catalogs, scissors, stickers and tape so friends can create their own handmade cards to mail out. To learn more and register, go to theangelcardproject.com.

Cookie Swap Sips & Snacks

It's party time! Serve up these festive (and easy) drinks and apps to nibble alongside guests' sweet treats.

GINGERBREAD EGGNOG

Active Time 25 minutes **Total Time** 1 hour 15 minutes **Serves** 16

- 1 cup heavy cream
- 1 1-inch piece fresh ginger, sliced
- 2 teaspoons pure vanilla extract
- 8 whole cloves, crushed
- 6 allspice berries, crushed
- 2 cinnamon sticks, broken
- ¼ teaspoon freshly grated nutmeg, plus more for serving
- 4 cups whole milk, divided
- 8 large eggs, separated
- ¾ cup sugar
  Pinch kosher salt
- ¾ to 1 cup dark rum, cognac, bourbon or a combination

1. In a medium saucepan, combine cream, ginger, vanilla, cloves, allspice, cinnamon, nutmeg and 2 cups milk. Cook on medium until tiny bubbles begin to appear around the edge of the pot (do not let boil), 2 to 3 minutes. Remove from heat and let steep 30 minutes.

2. Meanwhile, using an electric mixer, beat egg yolks in a large bowl on medium speed until combined. Gradually beat in sugar and salt. Increase speed to high and beat until thick and very pale in color, 2 to 3 minutes.

3. Strain spiced cream mixture, discarding spices; return to the pot. Slowly whisk 1 cup warm cream mixture into yolk-sugar mixture on low speed; return to pot with cream mixture. Cook on medium, stirring constantly with a rubber spatula until mixture reaches 170°F and coats the spatula, 12 to 15 minutes.

4. Place the pot over a large bowl filled with ice water and let cool, stirring occasionally, until chilled, 20 to 30 minutes. Stir in rum, cognac, bourbon or a combination and remaining 2 cups milk.

5. Just before serving, using an electric mixer, beat egg whites in a large bowl on medium-high speed until soft peaks form, 1 to 2 minutes. Fold into eggnog. Serve topped with nutmeg.

EASY UPGRADE

Give cheese a glow-up for the holidays. Take your favorite cookie cutter and press a shape into a **soft-rind cheese like Brie**. Then use a paring knife to score ⅛-inch down to outline the shape and use the tip of the knife to lift off the rind. Spoon your favorite **jam**, **honey** or **honey mustard** into the cutout or fill in with **finely chopped pistachios**, **pomegranate arils** or **dried cranberries**.

SPARKLING POMEGRANATE PUNCH

Active Time 15 minutes
Total Time 15 minutes, plus freezing
Serves 8 to 10

3	small Bartlett pears, divided
½	cup pomegranate arils, plus more for serving
¾	cup brandy
¼	cup pure maple syrup
3½	cups pomegranate juice, chilled
1	cup tangerine juice
2	tangerines
1	bottle sparkling white wine, chilled

1. Halve and core 2 pears, then thinly slice and scatter in a Bundt pan along with pomegranate arils. Fill two-thirds of the way with water and freeze until solid.

2. In a punch bowl, stir together brandy and maple syrup to dissolve. Add pomegranate and tangerine juices and stir to combine.

3. Thinly slice tangerines into rounds. Core and thinly slice remaining pear lengthwise. Add to the punch bowl.

4. Add ice ring to the punch bowl, then top with sparkling wine. Ladle into ice-filled glasses, spooning in fruit as desired.

How the Cookie Doesn't Crumble

Don't let all your hard work go to pieces while transporting your treats. Follow these tips for carrying them around the corner to a swap or shipping them across the country.

IF YOU'RE BRINGING THEM

Cut and store bar cookies in the pan they were baked in; cover the pan with foil or plastic wrap, then arrange cookies on a plate when you get there. (Some 9- by 13-inch pans even come with convenient snap-on plastic lids.)

For cookies coated with confectioners' sugar, dust them just before you leave, otherwise the sugar will be absorbed and the cookies will lose their sheen.

If you're transporting decorated sugar cookies or gingerbread cutouts, make sure to arrange them with wax paper between the layers to protect the pretty designs. The same goes for cookies with sugar glazes or sticky fillings.

IF YOU'RE SHIPPING THEM

Avoid fragile, buttery cutouts, or you may wind up with Christmas tree stumps and reindeer without antlers. Opt for sturdier varieties, such as drop cookies or bar cookies.

Use a durable cardboard box, plastic storage container or metal tin lined with impact-absorbing bubble wrap, foam peanuts popcorn or crumpled wax paper.

Wrap each cookie individually or in pairs back-to-back with plastic wrap or foil, and place in a resealable plastic bag for additional protection. If you're sending crisp cookies, don't pack them with softer ones—they'll absorb moisture and get soggy.

Seal the container with tape and place in a heavyweight box; fill in the space around the container with crumpled newspaper or bubble wrap. Clearly mark "fragile" and "perishable" in big letters on the outside of the package on all sides.

Plan ahead: Cookies shipped on a Thursday will sit in a warehouse all weekend, so mail early in the week; packages sent to soldiers overseas must conform to specific military and postal requirements (check usps.com or anysoldier.com for mailing instructions).

For optimal freshness, consider springing for overnight shipping.

Stock the Freezer

Gift yourself a collection of cookies you can enjoy all season long with these easy tips and best practices.

FRAGILE COOKIES

Tuck very buttery or crumbly cookies between layers of wax paper in airtight freezer containers.

STURDY COOKIES

Wrap stacks of four or five gingerbread, shortbread or biscotti in foil or wax paper, then place in freezer bags.

DECORATED COOKIES

Freeze in a single layer on a baking sheet until firm, then pack between layers of wax paper in airtight freezer containers.

BAR COOKIES

Wrap the whole batch uncut in foil or cut into bars and wrap individually in foil or wax paper, then place in freezer bags. Or leave bars cut or uncut in the pan and cover with plastic wrap or foil.

RAZZ JAMMY
THUMBPRINTS
page 27

CHAPTER 2

HOLIDAY HITS

These sweet treats are favorites for a reason. From Linzer Stars to Walnut Crescents and everything in between, these delicious go-tos are filled with the comforting tastes and textures of the happiest holiday memories.

Linzer Stars

Active Time 40 minutes | **Total Time** 1 hour, plus freezing and cooling | **Makes** 30

¾ cup pecans

1½ cups all-purpose flour, divided

½ teaspoon ground cinnamon

¼ teaspoon kosher salt

   Pinch ground cloves

   Pinch ground allspice

½ cup (1 stick) unsalted butter, at room temperature

½ cup granulated sugar

1 large egg, at room temperature

1 12-ounce jar seedless red jam

   Confectioners' sugar, for dusting

1. In a food processor, pulse pecans and 2 tablespoons flour until mixture resembles fine crumbs. Add cinnamon, salt, cloves, allspice and remaining flour and pulse to combine; set aside.

2. Using an electric mixer, beat butter and granulated sugar in a large bowl until light and fluffy, about 3 minutes. Beat in egg. Reduce mixer speed to low and gradually beat in pecan-flour mixture until combined.

3. Divide dough in half. Roll each half between 2 sheets of parchment paper to ⅛ inch thick. Freeze until firm, about 30 minutes.

4. Heat oven to 350°F. Line 2 baking sheets with parchment paper. Working with 1 sheet of dough at a time, use a floured 2-inch star cookie cutter to cut out cookies and transfer them to the prepared baking sheets. Reroll, chill and cut scraps.

5. With 1 sheet of cookies, use floured ½-inch star cookie cutter to stamp out shapes. Bake until edges begin to brown, 11 to 15 minutes. Let cool completely on the baking sheets.

6. Spoon about 1 teaspoon jam onto each whole cookie; dust stamped-out cookies with confectioners' sugar, then place 1 on top of each jam cookie.

SWEET SANDWICH

This traditional Austrian cookie is typically filled with raspberry or apricot jam. For a smooth bite, opt for seedless jams or jellies and avoid preserves, which contain chunks of fruit.

Walnut Crescents

Active Time 30 minutes
Total Time 50 minutes, plus chilling and cooling
Makes 45

1	cup walnuts
¾	teaspoon ground cardamom
1	cup confectioners' sugar, divided
1	cup (2 sticks) cold unsalted butter, cut into small pieces
2	teaspoons pure vanilla extract
2	cups all-purpose flour
½	teaspoon kosher salt
⅛	teaspoon ground cinnamon

1. In a food processor, pulse walnuts, cardamom and ¾ cup confectioners' sugar until walnuts are finely ground. Add butter and process until smooth. Mix in vanilla. Add flour and salt and pulse to combine. Shape into 1-inch-diameter logs and wrap in plastic. Refrigerate until firm, at least 1 ½ hours.

2. Line 2 baking sheets with parchment paper. Cut off a 1-inch-thick piece of dough, then roll into a 3 ½-inch log with tapered ends and bend into a crescent shape. Repeat with the remaining dough. Place crescents 1 ½ inches apart on the prepared baking sheets. Freeze until firm, about 20 minutes.

3. Heat oven to 350°F. Bake, rotating the positions of the baking sheets halfway through, until cookies are set and just barely turning golden brown around edges, 15 to 18 minutes. Let cool completely on the baking sheets.

4. In a large bowl, combine cinnamon and remaining ¼ cup confectioners' sugar. Liberally dust cookies with cinnamon sugar before serving.

Holiday Spritz Cookies

Active Time 25 minutes | **Total Time** 1 hour, plus cooling | **Makes** 72

1¼ cups all-purpose flour

¼ teaspoon kosher salt

½ cup (1 stick) unsalted butter,
at room temperature

¼ cup granulated sugar

1 large egg yolk, at room temperature

½ teaspoon pure vanilla extract

Red and green gel food coloring,
if desired

Royal Icing (page 8)

Sprinkles, for decorating

PRESS ON

If you're not a pro
at decorating cookies,
these Scandinavian-
inspired treats
are a savior. Every
squeeze of the press
creates a picture-
perfect cookie.

1. Heat oven to 350°F. In a medium bowl, whisk together flour and salt; set aside.

2. Using an electric mixer, beat butter and sugar in a large bowl on high speed until light and fluffy, 4 to 6 minutes. Reduce speed to medium, add egg yolk and vanilla, and beat for 5 minutes.

3. Reduce speed to low and gradually add flour mixture, mixing until just incorporated. Then, using a spatula, fold dough until it forms a ball. If desired, use food coloring to tint some or all of dough.

4. Fill a cookie press with dough according to the manufacturer's instructions. Hold the cookie press so it touches the baking sheet (do not line or grease the baking sheet), then squeeze and lift away, spacing cookies 1 inch apart. (You will need at least 2 large baking sheets.)

5. Bake, rotating the positions of the baking sheets halfway through, until light golden brown around edges, 11 to 13 minutes. Let cool on baking sheets for 1 minute before transferring to a wire rack to cool completely.

6. While cookies cool, prepare the Royal Icing. Decorate cooled cookies with icing and sprinkles as desired.

Minty Chocolate-Dipped Candy Canes

Active Time 35 minutes | **Total Time** 50 minutes, plus chilling and cooling | **Makes** 65 (depending on size and shape)

2 ¾ cups all-purpose flour

½ teaspoon baking powder

¼ teaspoon kosher salt

1 cup (2 sticks) unsalted butter, at room temperature

¾ cup sugar

1 large egg

1 ½ teaspoons pure vanilla extract

4 ounces semisweet or white chocolate

¼ teaspoon pure peppermint extract

Red and white nonpareils

1. In a large bowl, whisk together the flour, baking powder and salt; set aside.

2. Using an electric mixer, beat butter and sugar in a large bowl until light and fluffy, about 3 minutes. Beat in the egg and then the vanilla.

3. Reduce mixer speed to low and gradually beat in flour mixture until just incorporated. Shape the dough into 4 disks and roll each between 2 sheets of wax paper to ⅛ inch thick. Chill until firm, 30 minutes in the refrigerator or 15 minutes in the freezer.

4. Heat oven to 350°F. Line 2 baking sheets with parchment paper. Using floured candy cane cookie cutters, cut out cookies. Place on the prepared baking sheets. Reroll, chill, and cut the scraps.

5. Bake, rotating the positions of the baking sheets halfway through, until the cookies are golden brown around the edges, 10 to 12 minutes. Let cool on the baking sheets for 5 minutes before transferring to wire racks to cool completely.

6. Melt chocolate according to package directions, then stir in peppermint extract. Dip half of each cookie in chocolate, letting any excess drip off. Place on a wire rack set over parchment paper and sprinkle with nonpareils, if desired.

Classic Chewy Sugar Cookies

Active Time 20 minutes
Total Time 30 minutes, plus chilling and cooling
Makes 22

1 3/4	cups all-purpose flour
3/4	teaspoon baking powder
1/2	teaspoon baking soda
1/2	teaspoon kosher salt
1/2	cup (1 stick) unsalted butter, at room temperature
3/4	cup sugar
1	large egg, at room temperature
1/2	teaspoon pure almond extract
1/2	teaspoon pure vanilla extract

Switch It Up
FUN VARIATIONS

Try rolling dough balls in sprinkles or cinnamon-sugar before baking.

1. Heat oven to 350°F. Line 2 baking sheets with parchment paper. In a large bowl, whisk together flour, baking powder, baking soda and salt; set aside.

2. Using an electric mixer, beat butter and sugar in a large bowl on medium speed until light and fluffy, 1 to 2 minutes. Beat in egg until combined. Beat in almond and vanilla extracts. Reduce mixer speed to low and gradually beat in flour mixture until just incorporated. (The dough will be a little soft.) Freeze until firm, about 30 minutes.

3. Scoop dough onto the prepared baking sheets (about 1 1/2 tablespoons each), arranging them 2 inches apart. Bake until crisp around the edges, 10 to 12 minutes. Cool on the baking sheets 5 minutes, then transfer to wire racks to cool completely.

Chocolate-Pistachio Slice & Bakes

Active Time 20 minutes | **Total Time** 30 minutes, plus chilling | **Makes** 40

1 cup all-purpose flour

½ cup unsweetened cocoa

¼ teaspoon baking soda

¼ teaspoon kosher salt

½ cup (1 stick) unsalted butter, at room temperature

½ cup sugar

2 teaspoons pure vanilla extract

1 large egg

½ cup shelled unsalted pistachios, chopped

1. In a medium bowl, whisk together flour, cocoa, baking soda and salt; set aside.

2. Using an electric mixer, beat butter and sugar on medium speed until light and fluffy, about 3 minutes. Reduce speed to low and beat in vanilla and egg to combine. Add flour mixture, beating until just incorporated.

3. Divide dough in half. Using a piece of plastic wrap to guide, roll the dough into 2 logs, each about 8 inches long and 1 ½ inches in diameter. Roll the logs in pistachios to coat evenly, then wrap each in a piece of plastic wrap. Refrigerate until firm, at least 1 hour.

4. Heat oven to 350°F. Line 2 baking sheets with parchment paper. Slice dough crosswise into ¼-inch-thick rounds; transfer to the baking sheets, spacing them 2 inches apart.

5. Bake until tops feel sandy to the touch, 11 to 13 minutes. Let cool on baking sheets for 2 minutes before transferring to a wire rack to cool completely.

Switch It Up

CHOCO-NUT

Not a fan of pistachios? Roll this dough in any chopped nuts, such as walnuts or cashews.

Choco-Mint Snowflakes

Active Time 30 minutes | **Total Time** 45 minutes, plus chilling and cooling | **Makes** 48 (depending on size and shape)

2 ½   cups all-purpose flour

⅔   cup unsweetened cocoa

½   teaspoon baking powder

¼   teaspoon kosher salt

1   cup (2 sticks) unsalted butter, at room temperature

¾   cup sugar

1   large egg

1 ½   teaspoons pure vanilla extract

4   ounces white chocolate, melted

Crushed peppermint candies, for decorating

1. In a large bowl, whisk together flour, cocoa powder, baking powder and salt; set aside.

2. Using an electric mixer, beat butter and sugar in another large bowl until light and fluffy, about 3 minutes. Beat in egg and then vanilla. Reduce mixer speed to low and gradually add flour mixture, mixing just until incorporated. Shape dough into 2 disks and roll each between 2 sheets of waxed paper to ⅛ inch thick. Chill until firm, 30 minutes in refrigerator or 15 minutes in freezer.

3. Heat oven to 350°F. Line 2 baking sheets with parchment paper. Using floured cookie cutters, cut out cookies. Place on prepared baking sheets. Reroll, chill and cut scraps.

4. Bake, rotating the positions of the baking sheets halfway through, until cookies are light golden brown around edges, 10 to 12 minutes. Let cool on baking sheets 5 minutes before transferring to wire racks set over parchment paper or foil to cool completely. Drizzle cookies with melted white chocolate, then sprinkle with crushed peppermint candies while chocolate is still wet and let set before serving.

Razz Jammy Thumbprints

Active Time 25 minutes
Total Time 40 minutes, plus cooling
Makes 36

2 ¼   cups all-purpose flour

1   teaspoon baking powder

½   teaspoon baking soda

¾   cup (1 ½ sticks) unsalted butter, at room temperature

¾   cups granulated sugar

½   teaspoon kosher salt

1   large egg yolk

2   tablespoons honey

1   teaspoon pure almond extract

½   teaspoon pure vanilla extract

½   cup seedless raspberry jam

¼   cup confectioners' sugar, optional

1. Heat oven to 375°F. Line 2 baking sheets with parchment paper. In a medium bowl, whisk flour, baking powder and baking soda; set aside.

2. Using an electric mixer, beat butter, granulated sugar and salt in a large bowl on medium-high speed until creamy, 3 minutes. Beat in egg yolk, then honey and extracts until smooth, stopping and scraping down the side of the bowl occasionally. Reduce speed to low, then mix in flour mixture until smooth.

3. Roll tablespoonfuls of dough into balls and place onto the prepared sheets, spacing them 2 inches apart. With a floured finger or the rounded end of a small spoon, make an indentation in the center of each ball. Fill each indentation with ½ teaspoon jam. Bake until golden brown around edges, 12 minutes.

4. Let cool on baking sheets for 5 minutes before transferring to a wire rack to cool completely. Sift confectioners' sugar over cooled cookies if desired. Cookies can be stored in airtight containers in the freezer for up to a month.

Switch It Up

SALTED CARAMEL

Bake cookies unfilled. Once cooled, fill with dulche de leche and top with flaky sea salt.

NUT-ROLLED

After forming balls in step 2, roll in finely chopped walnuts or pecans. Fill and bake as directed.

Cranberry Shortbread

Active Time 20 minutes
Total Time 1 hour 20 minutes
Makes 28

- ⅓ cup sugar
- ¼ teaspoon chopped fresh rosemary
- ⅓ cup frozen cranberries (about 1 ½ ounces)
- ¾ cup (1 ½ sticks) unsalted butter, at room temperature
- ½ teaspoon pure vanilla extract
- 1 teaspoon finely grated orange zest
- 1½ cups all-purpose flour
- ¼ teaspoon kosher salt

1. Line 2 baking sheets with parchment paper. In a food processor, pulse sugar and rosemary until very finely chopped. Transfer to a large bowl. Wipe out the bowl of the processor, add frozen cranberries and pulse to break up into pea-size pieces.

2. Using an electric mixer, beat butter and rosemary sugar on medium speed until very well combined, 1 to 2 minutes. Beat in vanilla and zest.

3. Reduce speed to low and gradually add flour and salt, mixing until just incorporated. Add chopped cranberries and mix to combine. Dough should look streaky with bits of cranberries.

4. On a piece of plastic wrap, form dough into a 7 ½- by 2 ¾- by 1-inch-thick rectangle. Chill dough until firm, about

45 minutes in the freezer or 2 hours in the fridge.

5. Heat oven to 325°F. Slice dough crosswise into ¼-inch-thick rectangles; transfer to the baking sheets, spacing them 2 inches apart. Bake, rotating the positions of the baking sheets halfway through, until light golden brown around edges, 15 to 18 minutes. Let cool completely on the baking sheets.

Spiced Drops

Active Time 35 minutes | **Total Time** 55 minutes, plus chilling and cooling | **Makes** 42

2 ¼ cups all-purpose flour

2 ½ teaspoons ground cinnamon

2 teaspoons ground ginger

¼ teaspoon ground cloves

1 teaspoon baking powder

½ teaspoon baking soda

¾ cups (1 ½ sticks) unsalted butter, at room temperature

¾ cups granulated sugar

½ teaspoon kosher salt

1 large egg yolk

2 tablespoons light corn syrup

1 ½ teaspoons pure vanilla extract

½ teaspoon pure almond extract

¼ cup coarse sugar

1. Heat oven to 375°F. Line a baking sheet with parchment paper. In a medium bowl, whisk flour, cinnamon, ginger, cloves, baking powder and baking soda; set aside.

2. Using an electric mixer, beat butter, sugar and salt in a large bowl on medium-high speed until light and fluffy, about 3 minutes. Beat in egg yolk, corn syrup and extracts. Reduce speed to medium-low and mix in flour mixture until just combined.

3. Place coarse sugar in a small bowl. Roll tablespoonfuls of dough into balls, then roll in sugar and place onto the prepared sheet, spacing them 2 inches apart.

4. Bake until edges are set, 15 minutes. Slide the parchment with cookies onto a wire rack to cool completely.

Nankhatai

Active Time | 45 minutes **Total Time** 1 hour 30 minutes | **Makes** 16

1 ½ cups whole-wheat flour, preferably stone-ground

⅓ cup semolina

1 teaspoon kosher salt

⅔ cup ghee, at room temperature, preferably homemade

¾ cup confectioners' sugar

½ teaspoon ground cardamom

½ teaspoon freshly grated nutmeg

1 heaping tablespoon shelled pistachios, roughly chopped

Switch It Up

CRUMBLY COOKIE

For a more tender version, replace ½ cup of the whole-wheat flour with chickpea flour.

1. In a small bowl, whisk together flour, semolina and salt; set aside.

2. Using an electric mixer, beat ghee, confectioners' sugar, cardamom and nutmeg in a large bowl on medium-high speed until lightened in color, 2 to 3 minutes. Reduce speed to low and mix in flour mixture until just combined (dough may be slightly clumpy, similar to pie dough). Transfer dough to a piece of plastic wrap and form into a 1-inch-thick disk. Wrap well and refrigerate until slightly firm, 15 minutes.

3. Heat oven to 350°F. Line 2 baking sheets with parchment paper. Roll dough into balls slightly less than 1 ½ inches in diameter (about 1 ounce each) and place onto the prepared sheets, spacing them 3 inches apart. Flatten each ball to ¾ inch thick (crackly edges are totally fine). If desired, using a sharp knife, make a cross indentation about ⅛ inch deep into each cookie. Press a few pieces of chopped pistachio into center of cookies.

4. Bake, rotating the positions of the baking sheets halfway through, until set and golden brown on bottoms, 14 to 18 minutes (Cookies will be more tender at 14 minutes. If you like a crunchier cookie, bake to the longer end of the range.) Transfer cookies to a wire rack and let cool completely.

Spiced Butter Cookies

Active Time 25 minutes | **Total Time** 1 hour 10 minutes, plus chilling and cooling | **Makes** 70

2	cups (4 sticks) unsalted butter, at room temperature
1½	cups sugar
2	large eggs plus 3 large egg yolks
2	teaspoons pure vanilla extract
5	cups all-purpose flour
1¼	teaspoon ground cinnamon
1	teaspoon kosher salt
¼	teaspoon ground allspice

1. Using an electric mixer, beat butter in a large bowl on medium-high speed. Beat in sugar, eggs and egg yolks and vanilla. Reduce mixer speed to medium-low and beat in flour, cinnamon, salt and allspice until combined.

2. For drop cookies, transfer to an airtight container. For cutout cookies, divide dough in half, form into 1-inch-thick slabs and cover tightly with plastic wrap. For slice cookies, use parchment paper to roll dough into logs. Chill dough at least 2 hours.

3. Heat oven to 350°F. Line 2 baking sheets with parchment paper. Form cookies as desired, either by rolling dough into balls, cutting dough with cookie cutters or slicing dough log, then transfer to the prepared sheet pans and refrigerate, about 20 minutes. Bake until light golden brown, 10 to 15 minutes, depending on cookie size. Transfer cookies to a wire rack to cool completely. Repeat with remaining dough.

Switch It Up

CHOCOLATE COOKIES

Reduce flour to 4 ½ cups and add ⅔ cup cocoa powder.

Red Velvet Cookies

Active Time 20 minutes
Total Time 45 minutes
Makes 30

2	cups all-purpose flour
½	cup Dutch process cocoa powder
1	teaspoon baking soda
1	teaspoon kosher salt
1	cup (2 sticks) unsalted butter, at room temperature
¾	cup packed brown sugar
½	cup granulated sugar
1	large egg
1	teaspoon red gel food coloring
2	teaspoons pure vanilla extract
2	cups semisweet chocolate chips

1. Heat oven to 350°F. Line 2 baking sheets with parchment paper. In a large bowl, whisk together flour, cocoa, baking soda and salt; set aside.

2. Using an electric mixer, beat together butter and sugars in a large bowl on medium speed until combined, about 3 minutes. Add egg, food coloring and vanilla, and mix until just combined.

3. Reduce speed to low and add flour mixture until just combined. Fold in chocolate chips.

4. Scoop heaping spoonfuls of dough onto the prepared sheets, spacing them 1 ½ inches apart.

5. Bake, rotating the positions of the baking sheets halfway through, until darker around edges, 9 to 12 minutes total.

6. Let cool on baking sheets for 5 minutes, then slide parchment (and cookies) onto wire racks and cool for at least 5 minutes more before serving.

Frosted Lemony Ricotta Cookies

Active Time 30 minutes
Total Time 1 hour, plus cooling
Makes 42

4	cups all-purpose flour
2	teaspoons baking powder
1	teaspoon kosher salt
1 ¾	cups granulated sugar
1	cup (2 sticks) unsalted butter, at room temperature
1	teaspoon lemon zest plus 3 tablespoons juice
1	15-ounce container ricotta cheese
2	large eggs
2	teaspoons pure vanilla extract
1 ¼	cups confectioners' sugar
½	teaspoon water
	Blue food coloring, for decorating
	Edible silver stars, for decorating

1. Heat oven to 350°F. In a large bowl, whisk flour, baking powder and salt; set aside.

2. Using an electric mixer, beat granulated sugar, butter and lemon zest in another large bowl on medium-high speed until creamy, 3 minutes. Add ricotta, eggs and vanilla, beating until combined, stopping and scraping down the side of the bowl occasionally. Mix in flour mixture until just smooth.

3. Line a large baking sheet with parchment paper. With a small cookie scoop (about 2 teaspoons), scoop dough into balls and

place onto the prepared sheet, spacing them 1 ½ inches apart. With your fingers, pat each down into a disk. Bake until bottoms are golden brown, 15 to 20 minutes. Let cool on baking sheet for 5 minutes before transferring to a wire rack to cool completely.

4. Make the glaze: In a medium bowl, stir together confectioners' sugar, reserved lemon juice and water, until smooth. Tint with food coloring to desired shade. Place in a small resealable plastic bag with one corner snipped off and drizzle all over cookies. Decorate with edible stars if desired. Let sit until set, about 30 minutes. Cookies can be stored in airtight containers in the freezer for up to a month.

Switch It Up

CHOCOLATE-GLAZED RICOTTA

Omit lemon in cookies. Instead of confectioners' sugar glaze, drizzle with melted dark chocolate.

Danish Butter Cookies

Active Time 25 minutes | **Total Time** 45 minutes, plus chilling and cooling | **Makes** 20 to 24

- 1 cup (2 sticks) unsalted butter, at room temperature
- ½ cup granulated sugar
- 1 large egg plus 1 large egg yolk
- 2 teaspoons pure vanilla extract
- ¼ teaspoon kosher salt
- 2 cups all-purpose flour

  White sparkling sugar, for sprinkling (optional)

1. Using an electric mixer, beat butter and sugar in a large bowl on medium speed, scraping down the bowl halfway through, until light and fluffy, about 3 minutes. Beat in egg and yolk, then vanilla and salt, scraping the bowl as needed. Reduce mixer speed to low, gradually add flour and mix until just combined.

2. Line 2 baking sheets with parchment paper. Transfer dough to a piping bag fitted with large star tip (#21 star tip for flower pattern; #8B open star tip for wavy pattern) and pipe 2-inch shapes on the prepared baking sheets, spacing 1 ½ inches apart. Refrigerate 30 minutes.

3. Heat oven to 350°F. Sprinkle cookies with sparkling sugar if desired and bake, rotating the positions of the baking sheets halfway through, until cookies are light golden brown around edges, 16 to 18 minutes. Let cool on the baking sheets 5 minutes, then transfer to wire racks to cool completely.

Chocolate Spritz Sandwiches

Active Time 40 minutes | **Total Time** 1 hour 10 minutes | **Makes** 40 (20 sandwich cookies)

FOR THE CHOCOLATE-PEPPERMINT GANACHE

- ½ cup heavy cream
- 4 ounces semisweet chocolate, finely chopped
- ¼ teaspoon pure peppermint extract

FOR THE COOKIES

- 1 cup all-purpose flour
- ¼ cup unsweetened cocoa powder
- ¼ teaspoon espresso powder
- ¼ teaspoon kosher salt
- ½ cup (1 stick) unsalted butter, at room temperature
- ⅓ cup sugar
- 1 large egg yolk, at room temperature
- ½ teaspoon pure vanilla extract

1. Make ganache: In a small saucepan, heat cream on medium, whisking constantly, until just bubbling at edges, 4 to 5 minutes. Pour over chocolate in a heatproof bowl and let sit 5 minutes. Add peppermint; gently whisk until melted and smooth. Refrigerate until set, 30 minutes.

2. Meanwhile, make cookies: Heat oven to 350°F. In a bowl, whisk together flour, cocoa powder, espresso powder and salt; set aside.

3. Using an electric mixer, beat butter and sugar in a large bowl on medium speed until light and fluffy, 3 minutes. Scrape the bowl; beat in yolk and vanilla. Reduce mixer speed to low and gradually add flour mixture until dough just comes together.

4. Transfer dough to a cookie press per manufacturer's instructions (in batches if necessary). Using 2 ungreased baking sheets and holding the cookie press so it touches the sheet, squeeze and lift away, spacing cookies 1 inch apart.

5. Bake, rotating the positions of the baking sheets halfway through, until the edges and tops are set and the surface is dry, 13 to 15 minutes. Let cool on the baking sheets 1 minute, then transfer to wire racks to cool completely, about 15 minutes. Repeat with any remaining dough (rinse baking sheets with cold water to help cool, then dry).

6. Transfer ganache to a piping bag and pipe on flat side of half of cookies. Top with remaining cookies.

SPRITZ SMARTS

To ensure that spritz cookies adhere to the baking sheets and maintain their shape, use a standard (not nonstick) baking sheet that is unlined and ungreased.

BONUS RECIPE

Homemade Chocolate-Hazelnut Spread

Swap out the peppermint-ganache for this cocoa-nutty spread. Heat oven to 375°F. Roast **1/2 cup hazelnuts** on a rimmed baking sheet for 10 minutes, shaking once or twice. Wrap hot hazelnuts in a towel and roll vigorously to remove peel; cool completely. In a food processor, process peeled hazelnuts and **1/4 teaspoon kosher salt** until mostly smooth and runny, about 8 minutes. In a medium bowl, melt **2 ounces chopped dark chocolate** in the microwave in 20-second intervals until melted and smooth; stir in **1/2 cup sweetened condensed milk** and **1 tablespoon light corn syrup**. Add chocolate mixture to pureed hazelnuts; pulse until just combined. Makes about 1 cup.

Florentines

Active Time 40 minutes | **Total Time** 1 hour | **Makes** 66

1 cup raw pecans
5 tablespoons unsalted butter
¼ cup packed dark brown sugar
¼ cup honey
⅓ cup all-purpose flour
¼ teaspoon kosher salt
¼ cup dried cranberries, finely chopped
¼ cup candied ginger, finely chopped
1 teaspoon finely grated orange zest
1 cup bittersweet chocolate chips

1. Heat oven to 375°F. Line 2 baking sheets with parchment paper. Using a food processor, pulse pecans until finely chopped but not powdery, with some small chunks remaining.

2. In a medium saucepan, combine butter, brown sugar and honey, and cook on medium, stirring occasionally, until butter has melted, sugar has dissolved and mixture is smooth, 8 minutes. Remove from heat and stir in flour and salt, then chopped pecans. Fold in cranberries, ginger and zest.

3. Drop leveled teaspoonfuls of batter onto the prepared sheets, spacing them 3 inches apart. Bake until golden brown, about 5 to 7 minutes. Let cool on baking sheets until set, about 8 minutes, before transferring to wire racks to cool completely. Repeat with remaining dough.

4. In a small bowl, microwave chocolate at 50 percent power in 30-second intervals, stirring in between, until melted and smooth.

5. Place cooled cookies on a piece of parchment paper and drizzle with melted chocolate. Let sit until chocolate is set.

CLASSIC CRISP

Chock-full of fruit and nuts, these delicate, chocolate-drizzled delights make cookie platters shine. For a perfectly thin and lacy bite, finely chop the dried cranberries and ginger to the same size as the processed pecans so the batter spreads evenly.

Chocolate Peppermint Cookies

Active Time 25 minutes
Total Time 40 minutes, plus freezing and setting
Makes 20 to 22

1 ¼   cups all-purpose flour

¼   teaspoon baking powder

¼   teaspoon kosher salt

½   cup (1 stick) unsalted butter, at room temperature

⅓   cup sugar

1   large egg yolk

½   teaspoon pure vanilla extract

¼   teaspoon pure peppermint extract

4   ounces dark chocolate, chopped

3   candy canes, crushed, for sprinkling

1. In a medium bowl, whisk together flour, baking powder and salt; set aside.

2. Using an electric mixer, beat butter and sugar in a large bowl on medium speed, scraping the bowl halfway through, until light and fluffy, 2 to 3 minutes. Beat in yolk, then vanilla and peppermint. Reduce mixer speed to low, gradually add flour mixture until just incorporated.

3. Turn out dough onto a piece of plastic wrap and shape into a 6-inch log. Wrap and freeze 30 minutes to 3 months. (If freezing longer, let thaw slightly at room temperature to ease slicing; cookies may need an extra 1 to 2 minutes of baking.)

4. Heat oven to 350°F. Line 2 baking sheets with parchment paper. Slice log crosswise 1/4-inch thick and transfer to the prepared baking sheets, spacing 2 inches apart. Bake, rotating the positions of the baking sheets halfway through, until cookies are light golden brown around edges, 12 to 15 minutes. Let cool on the baking sheets 5 minutes, then transfer to wire racks to cool completely.

5. In a small bowl, microwave chocolate in 20-second intervals, stirring in between, until melted and smooth. Dip cooled cookies halfway in chocolate, sprinkle with candy cane bits and return to the parchment-lined baking sheets. Refrigerate until set, at least 15 minutes, then refrigerate in an airtight container to keep chocolate from melting.

Glazed Almond Cutouts

Active Time 35 minutes, plus decorating
Total Time 1 hour 5 minutes, plus chilling, cooling and decorating
Makes About 48 depending on shape

2 ¾ cups all-purpose flour, plus more
       for dusting

½ teaspoon baking powder

½ teaspoon kosher salt

1 cup (2 sticks) unsalted butter,
    at room temperature

¾ cup granulated sugar

1 large egg

1 teaspoon pure almond extract

½ teaspoon pure vanilla extract

Decorator's Icing (page 9), for decorating

Food coloring

Sugar pearls, for decorating

Sanding sugar, for decorating

1. In a large bowl, whisk together flour, baking powder and salt; set aside.

2. Using an electric mixer, beat butter and granulated sugar in a large bowl on medium speed until light and fluffy, 3 minutes. Beat in egg and then almond and vanilla extracts. Reduce mixer speed to low and gradually beat in flour mixture until just incorporated.

3. Shape dough into 3 disks and roll each between 2 sheets of parchment paper to ⅛ to ¼ inch thick. Chill until firm, 30 minutes in the refrigerator or 15 minutes in the freezer.

4. Heat oven to 350°F. Line 2 baking sheets with parchment paper. Using floured cookie cutters, cut out cookies and place them onto the prepared sheets, spacing them 2 inches apart. Reroll, chill and cut the scraps.

5. Bake, rotating the positions of the baking sheets halfway through, until cookies are light golden brown around edges, 10 to 12 minutes. Let cool on baking sheets for 5 minutes before transferring to a wire rack to cool completely.

6. Tint icing with food coloring as desired; keep surface covered with plastic wrap. With small spatula or decorating bags with small writing tips, decorate cookies with icing (add warm water to thin as desired). Add sugar pearls and sanding sugar if desired. Cookies can be stored in airtight containers at room temperature (with wax paper between layers) for up to 1 week.

Switch It Up

PUMPKIN SPICE

Add 1 tablespoon pumpkin-pie spice to the flour mixture.

Double-Chocolate Peppermint Cookies

Active Time 40 minutes | **Total Time** 1 hour 10 minutes, plus cooling | **Makes** 72

1 ½   cups all-purpose flour

¼   cup unsweetened cocoa

1   teaspoon baking powder

¼   teaspoon kosher salt

1   12-ounce package bittersweet chocolate chips

½   cup (1 stick) unsalted butter, at room temperature

¾   cup granulated sugar

2   large eggs

6   tablespoons heavy cream

8   candy canes, smashed (about ¾ cup)

1. Heat oven to 350°F. Line 2 baking sheets with parchment paper. In a medium bowl, whisk together flour, cocoa, baking powder and salt; set aside.

2. In a small bowl, melt ½ cup chocolate chips in the microwave in 30-second intervals, stirring between each until melted and smooth. Using an electric mixer, beat butter and sugar in a large bowl on medium-high speed until light and fluffy, about 3 minutes. Beat in eggs, one at a time. Reduce speed to low and gradually add melted chocolate and then flour mixture, mixing until just incorporated. Fold in ¾ cup of remaining chocolate chips.

3. Drop rounded teaspoonfuls of dough onto the prepared sheets, spacing them 2 inches apart. Bake, rotating the positions of the baking sheets halfway through, until cookies are puffed and set, 8 to 10 minutes. Let cool on baking sheets for 2 minutes before transferring to a wire rack to cool completely.

4. In a medium bowl, microwave heavy cream until simmering, about 30 seconds. Add remaining ¾ cup chocolate chips to cream and let sit for 1 minute. Stir until chocolate is melted and mixture is smooth. Spread about ½ teaspoon chocolate mixture on top of each cookie; top with candy canes. Refrigerate until set, about 20 minutes.

Millionaire Shortbread

Active Time 40 minutes
Total Time 3 hours 25 minutes
Makes 32

Nonstick cooking spray, for the pan

1/2 cup confectioners' sugar

1 1/4 cups (2 1/2 sticks) unsalted butter, at room temperature

1/2 cup slivered almonds, toasted and finely chopped

2 cups all-purpose flour

1 teaspoon kosher salt

1 14-ounce can sweetened condensed milk

1 cup packed dark brown sugar

1/2 cup pure honey

3/4 cup heavy cream

2 teaspoons pure vanilla extract

8 ounces bittersweet chocolate, chopped

Flaky sea salt, for sprinkling

1. Heat oven to 350°F. Lightly coat a 9- by 13-inch baking pan with nonstick cooking spray. Line pan with parchment paper, leaving a 2-inch overhang on the two long sides; spray paper.

2. Using an electric mixer, beat confectioners' sugar and 3/4 cup butter in a large bowl on medium speed until light and fluffy, 1 to 2 minutes. Reduce speed to low and beat in almonds, flour and 1/2 teaspoon kosher salt until just combined. Press dough into the bottom of the prepared pan. Bake until golden brown, 25 to 28 minutes. Let cool completely in the pan.

3. In a medium saucepan, combine condensed milk, brown sugar, honey, 1/2 cup cream and remaining 1/2 teaspoon kosher salt and 1/2 cup butter. Cook on medium, stirring constantly, until a candy thermometer reaches 236°F, 24 to 26 minutes. Remove from heat; stir in vanilla. Immediately pour caramel over shortbread. Let sit at room temperature until set, 1 to 1 1/2 hours.

4. In a bowl, microwave chocolate and remaining 1/4 cup cream for 30 seconds; stir. Continue to microwave in 10-second intervals, stirring after each until melted and smooth. Pour melted chocolate over caramel and spread with an offset spatula. Sprinkle with sea salt. Freeze until set, 15 to 20 minutes. When ready to serve, use overhangs to transfer to a cutting board and cut into squares. Store, refrigerated, in an airtight container for up to a week.

Chocolate Chip Mandel Bread

Active Time 25 minutes | **Total Time** 1 hour 40 minutes | **Makes** 40

3 ¼   cups all-purpose flour

1   teaspoon baking powder

½   teaspoon kosher salt

1 ½   teaspoons ground cinnamon

3   large eggs

1   cup canola oil

1   teaspoon pure vanilla extract

1 ¼   cups granulated sugar

1   cup semisweet chocolate chips

1   cup walnuts, roughly chopped

1. Heat oven to 375°F. Line 2 baking sheets with parchment paper. In a medium bowl, whisk together flour, baking powder, salt and ½ teaspoon cinnamon; set aside.

2. Using an electric mixer, beat eggs in a large bowl on medium speed until foamy, about 3 minutes. Mix in oil, vanilla and ¾ cup sugar. Reduce speed to medium-low and gradually mix in flour mixture until fully incorporated. Fold in chocolate chips and walnuts.

3. In a shallow dish, combine remaining ½ cup sugar and 1 teaspoon cinnamon. Divide dough into 6 equal portions and shape each into a 2-inch-wide loaf. Roll in cinnamon-sugar mixture and transfer to the prepared sheets, spacing them 1 inch apart.

4. Bake until loaves are set and golden brown, 15 to 20 minutes. Let cool on baking sheets for 10 minutes before transferring to a wire rack to cool for 20 minutes more. Reduce oven temperature to 350°F.

5. Slice loaves on a slight diagonal into ¾-inch-thick pieces. Place cut side up on the baking sheets, spacing them ½ inch apart. Bake until light golden brown, 12 to 15 minutes. Let cool at least 5 minutes before serving.

LIGHT & CRUNCHY

Similar to biscotti, these classic Jewish cookies (also known as mandelbrot) are twice baked, making them long-lasting and perfect for dipping into coffee or tea.

Chunky Nut Butter Cookies

Active Time 15 minutes | **Total Time** 25 minutes | **Makes** 12

1	cup all-purpose flour
¼	teaspoon kosher salt
¼	teaspoon baking soda
⅓	cup plus 1 tablespoon nut butter (peanut, almond or cashew)
½	cup granulated sugar
⅓	cup packed light brown sugar
1	large egg
2	tablespoons cold water, plus more if necessary
1	teaspoon pure vanilla extract
¼	cup chopped nuts

1. Heat oven to 375°F. Line 2 baking sheets with parchment paper. In a medium bowl, whisk together flour, salt and baking soda; set aside.

2. Using an electric mixer, beat nut butter in a large bowl until smooth, about 1 minute. Mix in sugars, then add egg, 2 tablespoons water and vanilla, and beat until thick and glossy, 2 to 3 minutes.

3. Reduce speed to low, add flour mixture and mix until combined (if dough is crumbly, add 1 to 2 teaspoons water). Fold in nuts.

4. Drop 2 tablespoonfuls of dough onto the prepared sheets, spacing them 2 inches apart. Bake until puffed and turning golden brown around edges, 10 to 11 minutes. Transfer to a wire rack to cool completely.

Shortbread Bites

Active Time 1 hour 45 minutes | **Total Time** 2 hours 45 minutes, plus chilling and setting | **Makes** 96

2 cups (4 sticks) unsalted butter, at room temperature

2 cups confectioners' sugar

4 teaspoons pure vanilla extract

5 cups all-purpose flour

1 teaspoon kosher salt

Glazes and toppings, for decorating

1. Using an electric mixer, beat butter in a large bowl on medium-high speed until smooth, about 8 minutes. Add sugar and beat until light and fluffy. Beat in vanilla. Reduce mixer speed to low, add flour and salt and beat until combined.

2. Divide dough into 4 equal pieces and pat each into a square. Roll out each square between 2 sheets of lightly floured parchment paper to ¼-inch thickness. Transfer to a baking sheet, wrap tightly with plastic wrap and refrigerate 2 hours.

3. Heat oven to 325°F. Line 2 baking sheets with parchment paper. Remove and unwrap 1 dough square. Using a floured 1-inch square cookie cutter, cut out 24 cookies. Transfer to the prepared baking sheets, spacing cookies about 1 inch apart. Bake, rotating the positions of the baking sheets halfway through, until light golden brown and firm around the edges, 12 to 15 minutes. Transfer cookies to a wire rack to cool completely. Repeat with remaining dough squares.

4. Meanwhile, make your choice of glaze (see below). Dip cookies in glaze on a diagonal, then gently swipe bottom edge to remove excess. Sprinkle with toppings as directed. Set cookies on wire racks, place over a sheet of wax paper and let glaze harden completely overnight.

PICK YOUR GLAZE

Lemon Glaze In a small bowl, combine 1 ½ cups confectioners' sugar, 3 tablespoons fresh lemon juice and 1 ½ tablespoons corn syrup. Dip cookies as directed and sprinkle with 1 tablespoon lemon zest.

Almond Glaze In a small bowl, combine 1 ½ cups confectioners' sugar, 3 tablespoons milk, 1 ½ tablespoons corn syrup and ⅛ teaspoon pure almond extract. Dip cookies as directed and sprinkle with 1 tablespoon finely chopped toasted almonds.

Blackberry Glaze Press 1 cup frozen blackberries, thawed, through a fine-mesh sieve to extract juices. In a small bowl, combine 3 tablespoons blackberry juice, 1 ½ cups confectioners' sugar and 1 ½ tablespoons corn syrup. Dip cookies as directed.

White Chocolate-Pistachio Glaze In a medium bowl set over a pot of simmering water, melt 8 ounces white chocolate and 4 teaspoons vegetable shortening. Remove bowl from heat and stir in 4 teaspoons pistachio paste and ⅛ teaspoon fine sea salt. Allow mixture to rest for 1 minute. Dip cookies as directed and sprinkle with 1 tablespoon finely chopped pistachios.

Shortbread Cookies

Nan-e Berenji

Active Time 1 hour | **Total Time** 2 hours 5 minutes | **Makes** 30

1½ cups rice flour, preferably stone-ground

½ teaspoon kosher salt

½ cup (1 stick) unsalted butter, at room temperature

⅔ cup confectioners' sugar

½ teaspoon ground cardamom

1 egg yolk, at room temperature

1½ tablespoons rosewater

1 tablespoon milk

1 teaspoon poppy seeds

1. In a small bowl, whisk together rice flour and salt; set aside.

2. In a food processor, combine butter, confectioners' sugar and cardamom. Process until fully combined and lightened in color, scraping down side as necessary, 1 to 2 minutes. Add egg yolk, rosewater and milk, and pulse, scraping down side as necessary, until fully incorporated. Add rice flour mixture and pulse until a smooth dough has formed.

3. Transfer dough to a piece of plastic wrap and use wrap to form into a 1-inch-thick disk. Wrap well and refrigerate until slightly firm but not hard, about 45 minutes.

4. Heat oven to 300°F. Line 2 baking sheets with parchment paper. Remove dough from the refrigerator and divide in half; cover one half and return to the refrigerator. Roll the other half into 1-inch balls and place onto the prepared sheets, spacing them 2 inches apart. Flatten balls to ½ inch thick and use the side of a small spoon to make indentations in each cookie (approximately ⅛ inch deep), forming a pinwheel pattern.

5. Sprinkle with poppy seeds and bake, rotating the positions of the baking sheets halfway through, until just beginning to turn golden brown on bottom, 20 to 22 minutes. Transfer to a wire rack. Repeat with remaining dough and poppy seeds.

PATTERN PLAY

These delicious rice cookies hail from Persian and Iranian cultures where many use a traditional cookie stamp to make the pattern indentations on the top, but you can achieve a similar effect with the side of a spoon or fork.

Chinese Almond Cookies

Active Time 40 minutes
Total Time 1 hour 5 minutes
Makes 18

- ²/₃ cup whole almonds (about 4 ounces)
- 1 cup all-purpose flour
- ³/₄ cup confectioners' sugar
- 1 teaspoon baking powder
- 1 teaspoon baking soda
- ¹/₂ teaspoon kosher salt
- 4 egg yolks, at room temperature
- ²/₃ cup melted lard, cooled until barely warm
- 1¹/₂ teaspoons pure almond extract

1. Heat oven to 350°F. On a small rimmed baking sheet, roast almonds until fragrant and beginning to brown, about 10 minutes. Let cool completely. Reserve 18 almonds for topping cookies.

2. Place remaining cooled almonds in a food processor along with flour, confectioners' sugar, baking powder, baking soda and salt, and pulse until almonds are very finely ground, about 30 seconds; transfer to a medium bowl.

3. In a small bowl, whisk together 2 egg yolks, lard and almond extract. Add to the bowl with flour mixture, stirring until flour is incorporated and dough just comes together (do not overmix). Cover with plastic wrap, pressing to adhere to surface, and let dough rest, 20 minutes.

4. Line 2 baking sheets with parchment paper. Roll dough into 1¹/₄-inch balls and place onto the prepared sheets, spacing them 3 inches apart. Flatten balls to about ¹/₃ inch thick, molding any cracked edges slightly with fingers.

5. In a small bowl, whisk together remaining 2 egg yolks. Generously brush tops and edges of cookies with yolk. Press a reserved almond into center of each cookie and then bake, rotating the positions of the baking sheets halfway through, until golden brown on bottom and just beginning to turn golden brown on sides, 14 to 18 minutes. (Cookies will feel set when lightly touched but will still be soft at this point. They harden as they cool.) Let cool on baking sheets for 2 minutes before transferring to a wire rack to cool completely.

PERFECT PORTIONS

These traditional almond cookies are said to bring good fortune in the New Year. For even baking, use a scoop to make sure each ball of raw cookie dough is the same size.

MOCHA COCOA
COOKIES
page 58

WHITE
CHOCOLATE
RASPBERRY
THINS
page 74

CHAPTER 3

TRADITIONS WITH A TWIST

The tried-and-true is great, but how about something new?
These holiday classics with a twist are brilliant, like fruitcake-inspired
Kitchen Sink Cookies and Sourdough Snickerdoodles. You never
know — one might become your new favorite!

Glazed Sourdough Snickerdoodles

Active Time 30 minutes | **Total Time** 1 hour 15 minutes | **Makes** 18

FOR THE COOKIES

1	cup all-purpose flour
¼	cup whole-wheat flour
1	teaspoon cream of tartar
⅛	teaspoon kosher salt
½	cup (1 stick) unsalted butter, at room temperature
½	cup granulated sugar
¼	cup packed brown sugar
1	large egg
1	tablespoon buttermilk
½	teaspoon apple cider vinegar

FOR THE SPICED SUGAR

⅓	cup granulated sugar
1½	teaspoons ground cinnamon
1½	teaspoons ground ginger
¼	teaspoon freshly grated nutmeg

FOR THE SOUR CREAM GLAZE

1¼	cups confectioners' sugar
3	tablespoons sour cream

1. Line 2 baking sheets with parchment paper.

2. Make the cookies: In a medium bowl, whisk together flours, cream of tartar and salt; set aside. Using an electric mixer, beat butter and sugars in a large bowl on medium speed until light and fluffy, 3 minutes. Reduce speed to low and beat in egg, followed by buttermilk and vinegar. Mix in flour mixture until just incorporated.

3. Make the spiced sugar: In a small bowl, whisk together sugar, cinnamon, ginger and nutmeg.

4. Scoop rounded tablespoonfuls of dough, dropping dough into spiced sugar to coat completely before transferring to the prepared sheets. Freeze until firm, about 30 minutes.

5. Heat oven to 350°F. Bake, rotating the positions of the baking sheets after 9 minutes, until cookies are puffed and edges are light golden brown, 12 to 14 minutes total. Transfer to wire racks.

6. Prepare the glaze: In a small bowl, whisk together confectioners' sugar and sour cream. (At first it may not seem like there is enough liquid, but it will eventually come together.) Using the tip of a knife or a small piping bag, glaze cookies by drawing lines back and forth on a diagonal across the surface. Let glaze set.

Chai Tree & Snowflake Cookies

Active Time 25 minutes | **Total Time** 40 minutes, plus chilling and cooling | **Makes** 50

2 ¾   cups all-purpose flour

½   teaspoon baking powder

¼   teaspoon kosher salt

1 ½   teaspoons ground ginger

1   teaspoon ground cinnamon

½   teaspoon ground cloves

½   teaspoon nutmeg

½   teaspoon cardamom

⅛   teaspoon black pepper

1   cup (2 sticks) unsalted butter, at room temperature

¾   cup granulated sugar

1   large egg

1 ½   teaspoons pure vanilla extract

    Royal Icing (page 8), for decorating

1. In a large bowl, whisk together flour, baking powder, salt, ground ginger, cinnamon, cloves, nutmeg, cardamom and black pepper; set aside.

2. Using an electric mixer, beat butter and sugar in another large bowl on medium speed until light and fluffy, about 3 minutes. Beat in egg and then vanilla.

3. Reduce speed to low and gradually add flour mixture, mixing until just incorporated. Shape dough into 2 disks and roll each between 2 sheets of parchment paper to ⅛ inch thick. Chill until firm, 30 minutes in the refrigerator or 15 minutes in the freezer.

4. Heat oven to 350°F. Line 2 baking sheets with parchment paper. Using floured cookie cutters, cut out cookies. Place onto the prepared sheets, spacing them 2 inches apart. Reroll, chill and cut scraps.

5. Bake, rotating the positions of the baking sheets halfway through, until light golden brown around edges, 10 to 12 minutes. Let cool on baking sheets for 5 minutes before transferring to wire racks to cool completely.

6. While cookies cool, prepare the Royal Icing. Decorate cooled cookies with icing.

HOT TIP

Cool baking sheets in between batches to prevent dough from spreading. Run lukewarm water, then cold, over the backs of sheets to quickly bring down their temperature, then dry.

Lemon-Thyme Coins

Active Time 25 minutes
Total Time 40 minutes, plus chilling and cooling
Makes 24 to 48

2 3/4	cups all-purpose flour
1/2	teaspoon baking powder
1/4	teaspoon kosher salt
1	cup (2 sticks) unsalted butter, at room temperature
3/4	cup granulated sugar
1	tablespoon fresh thyme leaves, plus more for serving, optional
4	teaspoons finely grated lemon zest
1	large egg
1 1/2	teaspoons pure vanilla extract
2	cups confectioners' sugar
1/4	cup fresh lemon juice

1. In a large bowl, whisk together flour, baking powder and salt; set aside. Using an electric mixer, beat butter and sugar in another large bowl on medium speed until light and fluffy, about 3 minutes. Add thyme and 2 teaspoons lemon zest. Beat in egg, then vanilla. Reduce speed to low and gradually add flour mixture, mixing until just incorporated.

2. Shape dough into two 1 1/2-inch-diameter logs. Wrap in plastic and freeze for 20 minutes.

3. Heat oven to 350°F. Line 2 baking sheets with parchment paper. Slice dough crosswise into 1/8-inch-thick rounds; transfer to the baking sheets, spacing them 2 inches apart.

4. Bake, rotating the positions of the baking sheets halfway through, until light golden brown around edges, 10 to 12 minutes, let cool on baking sheets for 5 minutes before transferring to a wire rack to cool completely.

5. In a bowl, combine confectioners' sugar, lemon juice and remaining 2 teaspoons lemon zest. Spoon over cooled cookies. Sprinkle with additional thyme if desired.

FREEZE FOR LATER

Prep the dough through step 3, then wrap the logs tightly in plastic and freeze in a resealable freezer bag for up to 3 months. Thaw overnight in the fridge, then unwrap, slice, and bake as directed.

Cranberry-Pistachio Cornmeal Biscotti

Active Time 25 minutes | **Total Time** 1 hour 35 minutes | **Makes** 12

2 cups all-purpose flour, plus more
for dusting

½ cup yellow cornmeal

1 teaspoon ground ginger

½ teaspoon baking powder

½ teaspoon kosher salt

1 cup sugar

¼ cup canola oil

2 large eggs, at room temperature

1½ teaspoons pure vanilla extract

1 teaspoon finely grated orange zest

½ cup shelled pistachios

½ cup dried cranberries

Melted dark chocolate, for dipping

Melted white chocolate, for drizzling

1. Heat oven to 350ºF. Line a baking sheet with parchment paper. In a medium bowl, whisk together flour, cornmeal, ginger, baking powder and salt; set aside.

2. Using an electric mixer, beat sugar, oil, eggs, vanilla and zest in a large bowl on medium speed until smooth and fully combined, about 2 minutes.

3. Reduce mixer speed to low and gradually add flour mixture, beating until just fully incorporated (dough will be stiff). Mix in pistachios and cranberries.

4. On the prepared baking sheet, with floured hands, shape dough into ¾-inch-thick log about 12- by 4-inches. Flatten the top. Bake, rotating the position of the baking sheet halfway through, until light golden brown and the top begins to crack, 32 to 38 minutes. Let cool 15 minutes.

5. Using a serrated knife, slice the log on a slight diagonal ½ inch thick. Arrange the slices, cut sides down, on the same baking sheet in a single layer. Bake, flipping the biscotti halfway through, until golden brown, 6 to 8 minutes per side. Transfer to a wire rack to cool.

6. Dip 1 end of each biscotto in melted dark chocolate, then drizzle white chocolate (with spoon or piping bag) on dark chocolate.

Earl Grey Tea Cookies

Active Time 10 minutes
Total Time 45 minutes, plus chilling and cooling
Makes 48

2 ¾ cups all-purpose flour

2 tablespoons fine Earl Grey tea leaves

½ teaspoon baking powder

¼ teaspoon kosher salt

1 cup (2 sticks) unsalted butter, at room temperature

¾ cup granulated sugar

1 large egg

1 teaspoon grated orange zest

LOOSE LEAF TEA

Citrusy and bright British Earl Grey tea is a blend of bergamot extract and black tea. Can't find loose leaves? Cut open a traditional tea bag.

1. In a large bowl, whisk together flour, tea leaves, baking powder and salt; set aside.

2. In a food processor, process butter and sugar until smooth. Add egg and zest, and pulse to combine. Then add flour mixture and pulse to combine.

3. Transfer dough to a lightly floured surface and roll into 2 logs, about 2 inches in diameter. Wrap each in plastic wrap and chill for at least 30 minutes.

4. Heat oven to 350°F. Line 2 large baking sheets with parchment paper. Slice the logs crosswise into ⅛-inch-thick rounds; transfer to the baking sheets, spacing them 1 inch apart.

5. Bake, rotating the positions of the baking sheets halfway through, until light golden brown around edges, 14 to 16 minutes. Let cool on baking sheets for 5 minutes before transferring to a wire rack to cool completely.

Mocha Cocoa Cookies

Active Time 25 minutes | **Total Time** 40 minutes, plus chilling and cooling | **Makes** 48 (depending on size and shape)

2 ¼ cups all-purpose flour

½ cup unsweetened cocoa powder

2 teaspoons instant espresso powder

½ teaspoon baking powder

¼ teaspoon kosher salt

1 cup (2 sticks) unsalted butter, at room temperature

¾ cup sugar

1 large egg

1 ½ teaspoons pure vanilla extract

Melted chocolate, for dipping

1. In a large bowl, whisk together flour, cocoa powder, espresso powder, baking powder and salt; set aside.

2. Using an electric mixer, beat butter and sugar in a large bowl until light and fluffy, about 3 minutes. Beat in egg and then vanilla.

3. Reduce mixer speed to low and gradually mix in flour mixture until just incorporated. Shape dough into 2 disks and roll each between 2 sheets of wax paper to ⅛ inch thick. Chill until firm, 30 minutes in refrigerator or 15 minutes in freezer.

4. Heat oven to 350°F. Line 2 baking sheets with parchment paper. Using floured small gingerbread and star cutters, cut out cookies. Place on prepared baking sheets. Reroll, chill and cut scraps.

5. Bake, rotating the positions of the baking sheets halfway through, until edges are set, 10 to 12 minutes. Let cool on the baking sheets 5 minutes before transferring to wire racks to cool completely. Once cool, dip half of each cookie in melted chocolate and let set.

KEEP IT COLD

Chilling cookie dough in the refrigerator firms it up, which decreases the possibility of over-spreading. It not only ensures a thicker, more solid cookie but an enhanced flavor as well.

Matcha Spritz

Active Time 15 minutes
Total Time 40 minutes, plus cooling
Makes 36

½	cup (1 stick) unsalted butter, at room temperature
½	cup sugar
4	ounces cream cheese, softened
¼	teaspoon kosher salt
2	ounces white chocolate, melted
1	large egg
1	teaspoon pure vanilla extract
1½	cups all-purpose flour
1	tablespoon plus 1 teaspoon matcha green tea powder

Switch It Up
CREAM CHEESE SPRITZ

Omit matcha. Dip cooled
cookie in melted white chocolate,
if desired.

1. Heat oven to 350°F. Using an electric mixer, beat butter, sugar, cream cheese and salt in a large bowl on medium speed until smooth. Beat in white chocolate, egg and vanilla, stopping and scraping down the side of the bowl occasionally. Reduce mixer speed to low, and beat in flour and tea until just combined.

2. Transfer dough to a large piping bag fitted with a star tip. Pipe onto a large baking sheet into 2 ½-inch-round wreaths, spacing about 2 inches apart. Bake until golden brown around edges, 15 to 18 minutes. Let cool on the baking sheet 5 minutes, then transfer to wire racks to cool completely. Cookies can be stored in airtight containers at room temperature for up to 1 week.

Green Tea Cookies

Active Time 25 minutes | **Total Time** 35 minutes, plus chilling | **Makes** 24

1   cup all-purpose flour

1   tablespoon matcha green tea powder

¼   teaspoon kosher salt

½   cup (1 stick) unsalted butter,
     at room temperature

¼   cup sugar

     Melted semisweet and white chocolate,
     for dipping, optional

MERRY
& BRIGHT

Matcha is a powder
made from green tea
leaves. For the best
flavor and brightest
color, opt for high-
quality culinary
matcha powder when
baking. Save the
ceremonial-grade tea
for drinking.

1. In a medium bowl, sift together flour,
    green tea powder and salt; set aside.

2. Using an electric mixer, beat butter and
    sugar in a large bowl on low speed until
    combined and smooth, about 3 minutes.
    Add flour mixture and mix until dough
    comes together.

3. Divide dough in half, place each half on
    a piece of plastic wrap and shape both into
    1 ½-inch-thick logs. Place in plastic and
    refrigerate for at least 30 minutes
    and up to a week.

4. Heat oven to 350°F. Line 2 baking sheets
    with parchment paper. Slice dough
    crosswise into ¼-inch-thick rounds; transfer
    to the baking sheets, spacing
    them 2 inches apart.

5. Bake, rotating the positions of the baking
    sheets halfway through, until dough no
    longer looks raw and cookies are just barely
    set at edges, 8 to 9 minutes. Let
    cool completely on baking sheets on
    a cooling rack.

6. Once cool, dip half of each cookie into
    melted chocolate if desired, and let set.

TEST KITCHEN TIP

To melt chocolate, place chopped pieces in a bowl and microwave at 50 percent power, stirring at 30-second intervals. Chocolate will still hold its shape when partially melted, so be careful not to overheat.

Yuzu Crinkle Cookies

Active Time 35 minutes | **Total Time** 50 minutes, plus chilling and cooling | **Makes** 28 to 30

1 2/3 cups all-purpose flour

1 teaspoon baking powder

1/2 teaspoon kosher salt

3/4 cup granulated sugar

4 tablespoons unsalted butter, melted

2 large eggs

3 tablespoons yuzu juice

1/2 teaspoon pure vanilla extract

Yellow gel food coloring (optional)

1/2 cup confectioners' sugar

1. In a medium bowl, whisk together flour, baking powder and salt; set aside.

2. In a large bowl, whisk together granulated sugar, butter, eggs, yuzu juice, vanilla and 3 drops food coloring (if using) until smooth; fold in flour mixture until smooth. Cover the bowl with plastic wrap and refrigerate 30 minutes.

3. Line a baking sheet with parchment paper. Place confectioners' sugar in a small bowl. Working with a few at a time, drop heaping tablespoon of dough into sugar, then roll to coat and form each into ball; place on the prepared baking sheet. Refrigerate 30 minutes.

4. Heat oven to 350°F. Line a second baking sheet with parchment paper. Coat chilled cookie dough balls in confectioners' sugar once more and place on the prepared baking sheets, spacing 1 1/2 inches apart. Bake, rotating the positions of the baking sheets halfway through, until cookies are puffed, crinkled on surface and just set around edges, 9 to 11 minutes. Let cool on the baking sheets 5 minutes, then transfer to wire racks to cool completely.

CITRUS STAR
Yuzu is a tangerine-size citrus fruit that tastes super tart and slightly floral. Find it whole or as juice at Japanese grocery stores.

MORE ABOUT MATCHA

Unlike other forms of green tea, Japanese matcha doesn't get steeped in water but rather is added directly to lattes, smoothies, and sweet treats.

Matcha Snowballs

Active Time 20 minutes
Total Time 30 minutes, plus chilling and cooling
Makes 16 to 18

1	cup all-purpose flour
½	cup pecan halves, toasted
⅛	teaspoon kosher salt
3	teaspoons matcha green tea powder, divided
½	cup (1 stick) unsalted butter, at room temperature
1	cup confectioners' sugar, divided
½	teaspoon pure vanilla extract

1. In a food processor, pulse flour, pecans, salt and 1 teaspoon matcha until finely ground; set aside.

2. Using an electric mixer, beat butter and ½ cup confectioners' sugar in a large bowl on medium speed until creamy and smooth, 1 minute. Scrape down the bowl, then beat in vanilla. Reduce mixer speed to low and add flour mixture in 2 batches, beating until just incorporated. Cover the bowl and refrigerate 30 minutes.

3. Heat oven to 375°F. Line 2 baking sheets with parchment paper. Roll dough into 1 ¼-inch balls (each about 1 ½ tablespoons) and divide between the prepared baking sheets, spacing 2 inches apart. Refrigerate 30 minutes.

4. Bake, rotating the positions of the baking sheets halfway through, until cookies are set and just barely turning golden brown around edges, 9 to 11 minutes. Transfer to a wire rack to cool completely.

5. In a small bowl, whisk together remaining ½ cup confectioners' sugar and 2 teaspoons matcha. Sift matcha-sugar mixture on top before serving.

Candied Ginger & Citrus Kitchen Sink Cookies

Active Time 35 minutes | **Total Time** 1 hour | **Makes** 60

- 1 cup plus 2 tablespoons all-purpose flour
- ½ teaspoon baking soda
- ¼ teaspoon kosher salt
-   Pinch ground ginger
-   Pinch ground cloves
- ½ cup (1 stick) unsalted butter, at room temperature
- ⅔ cup packed brown sugar
- ¼ cup granulated sugar
- 1 large egg
- 1 teaspoon dark rum or pure vanilla extract
- ¾ cup chopped pecans
- 2 tablespoons chopped candied ginger
- 6 tablespoons chopped candied orange peel
- 6 tablespoons chopped pistachios

1. Line 3 baking sheets with parchment paper. In a medium bowl, whisk together flour, baking soda, salt and ground ginger and cloves; set aside.

2. Using an electric mixer, beat butter and sugars in a large bowl on medium speed until light and fluffy, about 3 minutes. Beat in egg, then rum (or vanilla), and mix for 2 minutes. Reduce speed to low and gradually add flour mixture until nearly combined. Add pecans, candied ginger and 4 tablespoons each orange peel and pistachios.

3. Scoop rounded teaspoonfuls of dough onto the prepared sheets, spacing them 1 ½ inches apart. Press remaining candied orange peel and pistachios into top of each cookie. Freeze until firm, about 15 minutes.

4. Heat oven to 375°F. Bake, rotating the positions of the baking sheets after 8 minutes, until edges begin to turn golden brown, 11 to 12 minutes total. Let cool.

FREEZE FOR LATER

Running short on time? Prep the dough through step 3, then freeze dough balls on a baking sheet in a single layer until solid and transfer to a resealable freezer bag for up to 3 months. Bake from frozen, adding a few minutes to the bake time.

Strawberry-Oatmeal Cookies

Active Time 30 minutes
Total Time 45 minutes
Makes 24

1½	cups old-fashioned rolled oats
1¼	cups all-purpose flour
½	teaspoon baking soda
¼	teaspoon baking powder
½	teaspoon kosher salt
4	tablespoons (½ stick) unsalted butter, at room temperature
¾	cup packed light brown sugar
¼	cup granulated sugar
1	large egg, at room temperature
½	cup unsweetened applesauce, at room temperature
1	tablespoon pure vanilla extract
2	cups (2 ounces) freeze-dried strawberries, finely chopped

1. Heat oven to 350°F. Line 2 baking sheets with parchment paper. In a small bowl, whisk together oats, flour, baking soda, baking powder and salt; set aside.

2. Using an electric mixer, beat butter and sugars in a large bowl on high speed until light and fluffy, about 3 minutes.

3. Reduce speed to low and beat in egg until fully incorporated, then add applesauce and vanilla.

4. Gradually add flour mixture, mixing until just combined. Fold in strawberries.

5. Scoop balls of dough, about 2 tablespoons each, onto the prepared sheets, spacing them 2 inches apart. Bake until golden brown around edges but still soft in the middle, 12 to 16 minutes. Let cool on baking sheets for 4 minutes before serving or transferring to a wire rack to cool.

BONUS RECIPE

No-Bake Strawberry-Chocolate Clusters

In a small bowl, microwave **8 ounces bittersweet chocolate chips** in 20-second intervals, stirring in between, until melted and smooth. Drop 15 teaspoonfuls melted chocolate onto a parchment-lined baking sheet. Top each with **3 freeze-dried strawberries**. Drop another spoonful chocolate onto each strawberry stack, letting chocolate drip down slightly. Sprinkle with **crushed freeze-dried strawberries** and refrigerate until set, 10 minutes.

Chocolate-Almond Spritz Cookies

Active Time 25 minutes | **Total Time** 1 hour, plus cooling | **Makes** 72

- 1 cup (2 sticks) unsalted butter, at room temperature
- 1 8-ounce package cream cheese, at room temperature
- 1 cup granulated sugar
- ½ teaspoon kosher salt
- 1 large egg yolk
- 1½ teaspoons pure vanilla extract
- 2½ cups all-purpose flour
- 5 ounces melted bittersweet chocolate
- ½ cup finely chopped almond slivers

1. Heat oven to 375°F. Using an electric mixer, beat butter, cream cheese, sugar and salt in a large bowl on medium-high speed until creamy, 3 minutes. Beat in egg yolk and vanilla. Reduce speed to low and add flour, mixing until just incorporated.

2. Transfer dough to a large piping bag fitted with a large open star tip. Pipe dough into 2-inch logs onto baking sheets, spacing them 2 inches apart.

3. Bake until deep golden brown around edges, 12 to 18 minutes. Let cool on baking sheets for 10 minutes before transferring to wire racks to cool completely.

4. When cool, brush one end of each cookie with melted chocolate, then coat in almonds. Transfer to a piece of parchment paper and let set.

Lime & Coconut Coins

Active Time 35 minutes
Total Time 50 minutes, plus chilling and cooling
Makes 120

2 ¾ cups all-purpose flour

½ teaspoon baking powder

¼ teaspoon kosher salt

1 cup (2 sticks) unsalted butter, at room temperature

¾ cup granulated sugar

1 large egg

1½ teaspoons pure vanilla extract

2 cups confectioners' sugar

¼ cup fresh lime juice

2 teaspoons grated lime zest

Toasted coconut, for serving

1. In a large bowl, whisk together flour, baking powder and salt; set aside.

2. Using an electric mixer, beat butter and sugar in a large bowl on medium speed until light and fluffy, about 3 minutes. Beat in egg and then vanilla. Reduce speed to low and gradually add flour mixture, mixing until just incorporated. Shape dough into 2 logs, each 1 ½ inches in diameter. Place in plastic wrap and freeze for 20 minutes.

3. Heat oven to 350°F. Line 2 baking sheets with parchment paper. Slice dough crosswise into ⅛-inch-thick rounds; transfer to the baking sheets, spacing them 1 inch apart.

4. Bake, rotating the positions of the baking sheets halfway through, until cookies are lightly golden brown around edges, 10 to 12 minutes. Let cool on baking sheets for 5 minutes before transferring to a wire rack to cool completely.

5. In a small bowl, whisk together confectioners' sugar, lime juice and lime zest. Spoon glaze over each cookie, then sprinkle with toasted coconut and let set.

FAST FIX
If you're short on time, start with a box of store-bought vanilla wafer cookies then frost with the glaze and top as directed.

Speculoos Dippers

Active Time 35 minutes | **Total Time** 55 minutes, plus chilling and cooling | **Makes** 28 to 30

1 ¾   cups all-purpose flour

1 ½   teaspoons ground cinnamon

½   teaspoon baking soda

¼   teaspoon kosher salt

¼   teaspoon ground ginger

¼   teaspoon freshly grated nutmeg

⅛   teaspoon ground cardamom

⅛   teaspoon ground cloves

¾   cup (1 ½ sticks) unsalted butter, at room temperature

⅓   cup packed dark brown sugar

¼   cup granulated sugar

1 ½   teaspoons pure vanilla extract

Speculoos cookie butter, for dipping

1. In a medium bowl, whisk together flour, cinnamon, baking soda, salt, ginger, nutmeg, cardamom and cloves; set aside.

2. Using an electric mixer, beat butter and both sugars in a large bowl on medium speed, scraping the bowl halfway through, until light and fluffy, about 3 minutes. Beat in vanilla. Reduce mixer speed to low and gradually add flour mixture until just incorporated. Turn out dough onto a piece of plastic wrap and shape into a 7- by 5-inch rectangle. Wrap and refrigerate 30 minutes.

3. Between 2 sheets of parchment, roll out dough to a rectangle ³⁄₁₆-inch thick. Remove top layer of parchment. Using a floured fluted pastry cutter, cut dough into 1- by 2 ½-inch rectangles without moving

cutouts. Slide the parchment with dough onto a baking sheet and freeze 20 minutes.

4. Meanwhile, heat oven to 350°F. Line a separate baking sheet with parchment paper and carefully arrange rectangles on top, spacing 1 inch apart. Bake, rotating the position of the baking sheet halfway through, until cookies are dry and matte, 14 to 16 minutes. Let cool on the baking sheet 5 minutes, then transfer to wire racks to cool completely. Serve cookies with cookie butter for dipping or spread cookie butter between cookies to make sandwiches.

SWEET TRADITION

These snappy spiced holiday cookies originated in Belgium, where, historically, children left their shoes out the night before St. Nicholas Day and woke to find them filled with speculoos and other gifts.

Fruitcake Crisps

Active Time 25 minutes
Total Time 40 minutes, plus chilling and cooling
Makes 50

2 ¾   cups all-purpose flour

½   teaspoon baking powder

¼   teaspoon kosher salt

1   cup (2 sticks) unsalted butter, at room temperature

¾   cup granulated sugar

1   large egg

1 ½   teaspoons pure vanilla extract

⅓   cup chopped candied citrus (orange and lemon)

⅓   cup chopped pistachios

½   cup dried cranberries

HOLIDAY POWER BARS

Early iterations of fruitcake were more like protein-packed snacks than cakes and were given to soldiers in ancient Rome before becoming moist cakes associated with weddings and wealth.

1. In a large bowl, whisk together flour, baking powder and salt; set aside.

2. Using an electric mixer, beat butter and sugar in another large bowl on medium speed until light and fluffy, about 3 minutes. Beat in egg and then vanilla.

3. Reduce speed to low and gradually add flour mixture, mixing until just incorporated. Fold in candied citrus, pistachios and dried cranberries. Shape dough into 2 logs, each 2 inches thick. Wrap and flatten slightly to create an oval; freeze for 20 minutes.

4. Heat oven to 350°F. Line 2 baking sheets with parchment paper. Cut logs into ½-inch-thick slices and place onto the prepared sheets, spacing them 2 inches apart.

5. Bake, rotating the positions of the baking sheets halfway through, until light golden brown around edges, 12 to 14 minutes. Let cool on baking sheets for 5 minutes before transferring to wire racks to cool completely.

Chocolate-Citrus Cran Wheels

Active Time 40 minutes | **Total Time** 1 hour 15 minutes, plus chilling and cooling | **Makes** 48

2 cups all-purpose flour

¼ teaspoon baking soda

¼ teaspoon kosher salt

¾ cup dried cranberries

½ cup confectioners' sugar

½ cup granulated sugar

¾ cup (1 ½ sticks) unsalted butter, at room temperature

1 teaspoon orange zest

1 teaspoon pure vanilla extract

¼ teaspoon ground cinnamon

Melted white or dark chocolate (about 12 ounces), for dipping

Dried orange slices, optional

1. In a medium bowl, whisk together flour, baking soda and salt; set aside.

2. In a food processor, pulse dried cranberries, confectioners' sugar and granulated sugar until cranberries are very finely chopped; transfer to a large mixing bowl.

3. Using an electric mixer, beat cranberry mixture and butter in a large bowl on medium-high speed until combined, about 1 to 2 minutes. Beat in orange zest, vanilla and cinnamon. Reduce speed to low and gradually add flour mixture, mixing until just incorporated.

4. Divide dough in half. Roll each half into a 2-inch-diameter log; wrap tightly with plastic. Refrigerate overnight or up to a week.

5. Heat oven to 350°F. Line a large baking sheet with parchment paper. Slice dough crosswise into ¼-inch-thick rounds; transfer to the baking sheet, spacing them about 1 inch apart.

6. Bake until golden brown around edges, 15 to 17 minutes. Let cool on baking sheet for 5 minutes before transferring to a wire rack to cool completely. Repeat slicing and baking with the remaining dough.

7. Dip cooled cookies halfway into melted chocolate; decorate with orange slices if desired. Place onto a parchment-lined baking sheet. Refrigerate until set, at least 15 minutes. Cookies can be stored in airtight containers in the freezer for up to 2 weeks.

Switch It Up

LEMON-APRICOT

Replace cranberries with ¾ cup coarsely chopped dried apricots. Use lemon zest instead of orange.

CHERRY-ALMOND

Replace cranberries with ¾ cup dried cherries. Add ½ teaspoon pure almond extract along with vanilla.

Shortbread Bars, 3 Ways

Active Time 10 minutes | **Total Time** 40 minutes | **Makes** 24

SHORTBREAD DOUGH

1 1/2 cups (2 1/2 sticks) unsalted butter, at room temperature

3/4 cup granulated sugar

1 teaspoon pure vanilla extract

3 cups all-purpose flour

1/2 teaspoon kosher salt

1. Heat oven to 350°F. Line a 9- by 13-inch baking pan with parchment paper, leaving a 2-inch overhang on the two long sides.

2. Using an electric mixer, beat butter and sugar in a large bowl on medium speed until combined, 2 minutes. Beat in vanilla.

3. Reduce speed to low and gradually add flour and salt, mixing until just incorporated. Press or spread mixture into the bottom of the prepared pan. Bake until light golden brown, 25 to 30 minutes. Let cool, then top as desired (see ideas, at right).

1

Chocolate–Peppermint Bars

Active Time 20 minutes
Total Time 55 minutes, plus chilling
Makes 24

1. Prepare **Shortbread Dough** as directed.

2. Using an electric mixer, beat **6 tablespoons unsalted butter** (at room temperature) in a large bowl on medium speed until smooth, 3 minutes. Reduce speed to low and gradually add **3 cups confectioners' sugar** until fully incorporated. Add **3 tablespoons heavy cream** and **1 1/2 teaspoons pure peppermint extract** and beat for 2 minutes. Spread over cooled crust and refrigerate until firm, at least 30 minutes.

3. In a medium bowl, melt **12 ounces semisweet chocolate chips** and **6 tablespoons unsalted butter** (cut into pieces) in microwave on 50 percent power in 30-second intervals, stirring after each interval, until melted and smooth. Spread onto peppermint layer and refrigerate until set, at least 30 minutes, before cutting into pieces.

2

Citrus Crumble Bars

Active Time 15 minutes
Total Time 55 minutes
Makes 24

1. Prepare **Shortbread Dough** as directed, but transfer 3/4 cup dough to a piece of plastic wrap, roll into a log and freeze until firm, 30 minutes.

2. Spread remaining dough into the pan and bake only 12 minutes; let cool completely.

3. In a small bowl, combine **1 cup red currant jam** with **2 tablespoons Grand Marnier** or other orange liqueur and **1 teaspoon finely grated orange zest**, and spread over dough.

4. Using a box grater, coarsely grate frozen dough over top. Bake until golden brown, 35 to 40 minutes. Let cool before cutting into pieces.

Toffee–Pecan Bars

Active Time 15 minutes
Total Time 55 minutes
Makes 24

1. Prepare **Shortbread Dough** as directed.

2. In a heavy-bottomed medium saucepan, combine **2 cups granulated sugar** and **1/3 cup water**. Heat on medium (do not stir), swirling the pan occasionally, until sugar has dissolved.

3. Increase heat and boil until sugar is a deep caramel color (do not stir). Immediately remove from heat and stir in **3/4 cup heavy cream** (it will bubble up), then fold in **4 cups toasted pecans**, very roughly chopped.

4. Pour mixture over cooled crust and sprinkle with **flaky sea salt**. Let cool before cutting into pieces.

White Chocolate Raspberry Thins

Active Time 25 minutes
Total Time 40 minutes, plus chilling and cooling
Makes 24 to 48

2 1/2 cups freeze-dried raspberries, plus more for serving

2 1/2 cups all-purpose flour

1/2 teaspoon baking powder

1/4 teaspoon kosher salt

1 cup (2 sticks) unsalted butter, at room temperature

3/4 cup sugar

1 large egg

1 1/2 teaspoons pure vanilla extract

White chocolate, melted, for serving

1. In a food processor, finely grind freeze-dried raspberries (you should have a scant 1/2 cup). In a large bowl, whisk together raspberry powder, flour, baking powder and salt; set aside.

2. Using an electric mixer, beat butter and sugar in another large bowl on medium speed until light and fluffy, 3 minutes. Beat in egg and then vanilla. Reduce speed to low and gradually add in flour mixture, mixing until just incorporated.

3. Shape dough into 2 logs. Using your hands or 2 clean rulers on the sides, press each log into two 2-inch-long squared-off logs. Place in plastic wrap and freeze for 20 minutes.

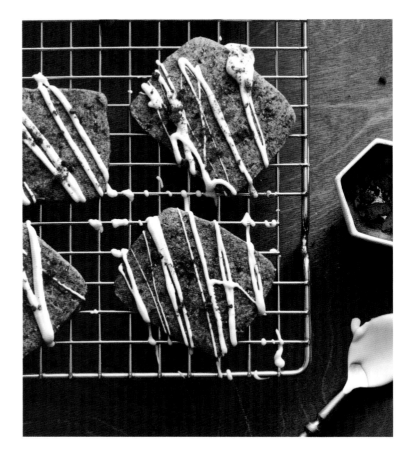

4. Heat oven to 350°F. Line 2 baking sheets with parchment paper. Slice dough crosswise into 1/8-inch-thick squares; transfer to the baking sheets, spacing them 2 inches apart.

5. Bake, rotating the positions of the baking sheets halfway through, until cookies are light golden brown around edges, 10 to 12 minutes. Let cool on baking sheets for 5 minutes before transferring to a cooling rack to cool completely.

6. Once cool, drizzle with melted white chocolate and sprinkle with crushed freeze-dried raspberries.

Pecan Snowflake Cookies

Active Time 40 minutes | **Total Time** 1 hour, plus chilling and cooling | **Makes** 36

- 1 **cup pecans**
- 1 **cup confectioners' sugar, divided**
- 1 **cup (2 sticks) cold unsalted butter, cut into small pieces**
- 1 **teaspoon pure vanilla extract**
- 2 **cups all-purpose flour, plus more for dusting**
- ½ **teaspoon kosher salt**
- ½ **teaspoon ground cinnamon**

1. Using a food processor, pulse pecans and ¾ cup sugar until finely ground, 10 to 12 times. Add butter and vanilla. Pulse until smooth, 14 to 16 times. Add flour, salt and cinnamon. Process until combined, 15 to 20 seconds. Roll between parchment paper to ¼-inch thickness. Chill until firm, 30 minutes or up to 2 days.

2. Heat oven to 350°F. Line 2 baking sheets with parchment paper.

3. Using a floured snowflake cookie cutter, cut out cookies and place on the prepared baking sheets, spacing 1 ½ inches apart. Bake until lightly golden brown around the edges, 7 to 10 minutes. Cool on the baking sheets on wire racks.

4. Dust with remaining ¼ cup confectioners' sugar.

REINDEER &
TREE SUGAR
COOKIES
page 82

CHAPTER 4

SHOW-STOPPING SWEETS

Gather your cookie construction crew and let the building begin!
These cookie creations include stuffed gingerbread s'mores,
iced chocolate mittens, red-and-white strawberry swirls,
plus some epic gingerbread homes.

Neapolitan Cookies

Active Time 40 minutes
Total Time 2 hours 50 minutes, plus cooling
Makes 14 to 16

1 ¼	cups all-purpose flour
¼	teaspoon baking powder
¼	teaspoon kosher salt
½	cup (1 stick) unsalted butter, at room temperature
½	cup confectioners' sugar
1	large egg yolk, at room temperature
¼	teaspoon pure vanilla extract
¼	cup freeze-dried strawberries (⅛ ounce)
½	teaspoon granulated sugar
	Red food coloring (optional)
1	ounce dark chocolate, melted and cooled to room temperature

1. In a medium bowl, whisk together flour, baking powder and salt; set aside.

2. Using an electric mixer, beat butter and confectioners' sugar in a large bowl on medium speed until creamy and smooth, 1 to 2 minutes. Scrape down the bowl, then beat in yolk and vanilla. Reduce mixer speed to low and gradually add flour mixture until just incorporated. Transfer two-thirds of dough to a second large bowl and set aside.

3. In a mini food processor, pulse strawberries with granulated sugar until finely ground (sift out any large pieces for 1 heaping tablespoon strawberry powder). Add to one-third dough in a large bowl and, using an electric mixer,

beat in 2 drops red food coloring (if using) on low speed until evenly colored. Transfer to a work surface.

4. Transfer half of remaining dough to a large bowl and, using an electric mixer, beat in melted chocolate until evenly colored.

5. On 3 separate sheets of plastic wrap, shape each piece of dough into 2- by 7-inch rectangle about ½ inch thick (if dough gets too soft, refrigerate a few minutes before proceeding), pressing a bench scraper along each side to straighten. Stack vanilla dough on strawberry, followed by chocolate and press into 1 long block with straight sides all around. Wrap tightly in plastic and refrigerate, striped side down, until very firm, 1 to 2 hours.

6. Heat oven to 350°F. Line a baking sheet with parchment paper. Using a sharp knife, slice the cookie block crosswise into ½-inch-thick cookies and place on prepared baking sheet, spacing 1 inch apart. Bake, rotating the position of the baking sheet halfway through, until cookies are set around edges and look dry and matte on surface, 12 to 14 minutes. Let cool on the baking sheet 5 minutes, then transfer to a wire rack to cool completely.

Chocolate-Dipped Cookie Sticks

Active Time 1 hour 5 minutes | **Total Time** 1 hour 25 minutes, plus cooling and chilling | **Makes** 26 to 28

FOR THE COOKIE STICKS

1 cup all-purpose flour, plus more for dusting

¼ teaspoon baking powder

¼ teaspoon kosher salt

5 tablespoons sugar

4 tablespoons unsalted butter, melted

2 tablespoons whole milk

1 large egg yolk

½ teaspoon pure vanilla extract

FOR THE COATING

4 ounces dark chocolate, finely chopped

¼ cup roasted almonds, finely chopped

¾ cup white chocolate chips

1 teaspoon coconut oil

Red and white nonpareils, for decorating

1. Heat oven to 350°F. Line 2 baking sheets with parchment paper. In a medium bowl, whisk together flour, baking powder and salt; set aside. In a second medium bowl, whisk together sugar, butter, milk, yolk and vanilla; fold into dry ingredients until combined and dough comes together.

2. Scoop ½-tablespoon portions of dough onto a lightly floured work surface and roll into 7-inch-long sticks (dough will initially be soft but will firm up as you work). Carefully arrange sticks on the prepared baking sheets, spacing 1 inch apart. Bake, rotating the positions of the baking sheets halfway through, until lightly golden and dry,

16 to 19 minutes. Let cool on the baking sheets 5 minutes, then transfer to wire racks to cool completely.

3. Line 2 baking sheets with fresh parchment paper. In a small bowl, microwave dark chocolate in 20-second intervals, stirring in between, until melted and smooth; transfer to a tall heatproof glass. Dip one-fourth of sticks (6 or 7) in chocolate, leaving 1 ½ inch of 1 end of each uncovered (tilt the measuring cup and spoon chocolate onto sticks as needed). Let excess chocolate drip off, gently scraping off excess with spoon if thick, then place on the prepared baking sheet and sprinkle with chopped almonds. Repeat with another one-fourth of sticks.

4. In an additional bowl, repeat melting with white chocolate, then stir in coconut oil; transfer to a second tall heatproof glass. Repeat coating the remaining cookie sticks in 2 batches, sprinkling with nonpareils after dipping each batch.

5. Refrigerate all sticks until set, at least 15 minutes, then refrigerate in an airtight container to prevent chocolate from melting.

SWEET STICKS

Inspired by Pocky, the iconic Japanese packaged snack, these crunchy sticks are very delicate once baked, so dip carefully.

Salted Chocolate Caramel Cookies

Active Time 1 hour 20 minutes | **Total Time** 2 hours 15 minutes | **Makes** 36

- 2 cups all-purpose flour
- 1⅓ cups unsweetened cocoa powder
- 2 teaspoons baking soda
- ¼ teaspoon salt
- 1 cup (2 sticks) unsalted butter, at room temperature
- ½ cup granulated sugar
- 1½ cups packed light brown sugar
- 2 large eggs, at room temperature
- 2 teaspoons pure vanilla extract
- ¼ cup buttermilk
- 12 ounces bittersweet chocolate, chopped (about 2 cups)
- 36 soft caramels
  Flaky sea salt

1. Line a baking sheet with parchment paper. In a medium bowl, sift together flour, cocoa powder, baking soda and salt, then whisk to combine; set aside.

2. Using an electric mixer, beat butter and sugars in a large bowl on medium speed until light and fluffy, about 3 minutes. Reduce speed to low and add eggs one at a time, then vanilla.

3. Add flour mixture in two parts, alternating with buttermilk and beating until just incorporated. Fold in chocolate chunks by hand and then refrigerate for at least 30 minutes.

4. Shape dough into balls (about 2 tablespoons each). Place balls onto the prepared sheet and refrigerate while preparing caramels. With the back of a spoon, flatten each caramel into a ¾-inch-wide disk. Then flatten each dough ball into a disk and wrap around a flattened caramel; return to the baking sheet and refrigerate.

5. Heat oven to 350°F. Line 2 baking sheets with parchment paper. Place chilled dough onto the prepared sheets, spacing them 2 inches apart. Sprinkle with sea salt and bake, rotating the positions of the baking sheets halfway through, until set around edges, 10 to 12 minutes. Let cool on baking sheets for 5 minutes before transferring to a wire rack to cool completely.

Switch It Up

CANDY CRUSH

Instead of regular caramels, try stuffing these decadent double-chocolate cookies with Rolos or peanut butter cups.

Jammy Sandwiches

Active Time 40 minutes
Total Time 1 hour, plus chilling and cooling
Makes 48

2 ¾ cups all-purpose flour

1 teaspoon ground cinnamon

½ teaspoon ground nutmeg

½ teaspoon baking powder

¼ teaspoon ground cloves

¼ teaspoon kosher salt

1 cup (2 sticks) unsalted butter, at room temperature

¾ cup granulated sugar

1 large egg plus 1 egg yolk

2 teaspoons pure vanilla extract

2 teaspoons finely grated orange zest

1 ½ cups apricot or raspberry jam
   Confectioners' sugar, for dusting

1. In a large bowl, whisk together flour, cinnamon, nutmeg, baking powder, cloves and salt; set aside.

2. Using an electric mixer, beat butter and sugar in another large bowl on medium speed until light and fluffy, about 3 minutes. Beat in egg and yolk, then vanilla and zest.

3. Reduce speed to low and gradually add flour mixture, mixing until just incorporated. Shape dough into 4 disks and roll each between 2 sheets of parchment paper to ⅛-inch thickness. Chill until firm, 30 minutes in the refrigerator or 15 minutes in the freezer.

4. Heat oven to 350°F. Line 2 baking sheets with parchment paper. Using floured 2- to 3-inch round fluted cutters, cut out cookies. Place cookies onto the prepared baking sheets, spacing them 2 inches apart. Using a smaller cutter, cut out centers from half the cookies. Reroll, chill and cut scraps.

5. Bake until cookies are light golden brown around edges, 10 to 12 minutes, rotating the positions of the baking sheets halfway through. Let cool on baking sheets for 5 minutes before transferring to a wire rack to cool completely.

6. Once cookies are cool, spread 1 ½ teaspoons jam onto each whole cookie. Dust cutout cookies with confectioners' sugar, then place on top of jam-covered cookies.

81

Sugar Cookie Creations

With just one basic dough and some imagination, you can build the most magical cookies. Start with our Classic Sugar Cookie Dough, then see where the season takes you.

Classic Sugar Cookie Dough

Active Time 10 minutes
Total Time 10 minutes, plus chilling
Makes 36 to 50 (depending on size and shape)

2 ¾   cups all-purpose flour

½   teaspoon baking powder

½   teaspoon kosher salt

1   cup (2 sticks) unsalted butter, at room temperature

¾   cup sugar

1   large egg

1 ½   teaspoons pure vanilla extract

1. In a large bowl, whisk together flour, baking powder and salt; set aside.

2. Using an electric mixer, beat butter and sugar in a large bowl on medium speed until light and fluffy, 3 minutes. Beat in egg and then vanilla. Reduce mixer speed to low and gradually beat in flour mixture until just incorporated.

3. Shape dough into 3 disks and roll each between 2 sheets of parchment paper to ⅛ to ¼ inch thick. Chill until firm, 30 minutes in the refrigerator or 15 minutes in the freezer.

Reindeer & Tree Sugar Cookies

Active Time 25 minutes
Total Time 40 minutes, plus chilling and cooling
Makes 50 (depending on size and shape)

1   batch Classic Sugar Cookie Dough (see left)

Red, green, white and gold Royal Icing (page 8)

Sanding sugars and sugar pearls, for decorating

1. Prepare Classic Sugar Cookie Dough as directed. Heat oven to 350°F. Line 2 baking sheets with parchment paper. Using floured reindeer and tree cookie cutters, cut out cookies and place them onto the prepared sheets, spacing them 2 inches apart. Reroll, chill and cut the scraps.

2. Bake, rotating the positions of the baking sheets halfway through, until cookies are light golden brown around edges, 10 to 12 minutes. Let cool on baking sheets for 5 minutes before transferring to a wire rack to cool completely.

3. Prepare Royal Icing as directed and decorate as desired.

Decorate Like a Pro

The details on these cutout cookies will take your treat tray to the next level.

GO METALLIC
Boost shimmer by dyeing Royal Icing (see page 8) with vibrant gold food coloring (available at craft stores), then piping it into the reindeer's antlers.

DOT ON DETAILS
Silver and gold candy balls (also called sugar pearls) add dimension to trees and reindeer noses. "Glue" to cookies using a small dot of Royal Icing. Remove before eating.

FINE-TUNE TREES
Flood trees with green royal icing and let set. Drop dabs of white icing on top, then use a small brush to drag upward for a snow-capped look.

Need a refresher on the basic techniques? Turn to page 9.

Polar Bear Sugar Cookies

Active Time 25 minutes | **Total Time** 40 minutes, plus chilling and cooling | **Makes** 50 (depending on size and shape)

1 batch Classic Sugar Cookie Dough (page 82)

1 batch Royal Icing (page 8)

Mini brown M&Ms, for decorating

1. Prepare Classic Sugar Cookie Dough as directed. Heat oven to 350°F. Line 2 baking sheets with parchment paper. Using floured bear cookie cutters, cut out cookies and place them onto the prepared sheets, spacing them 2 inches apart. Reroll, chill and cut the scraps.

2. Bake, rotating the positions of the baking sheets halfway through, until cookies are light golden brown around edges, 10 to 12 minutes. Let cool on baking sheets for 5 minutes before transferring to wire racks to cool completely.

3. Meanwhile, prepare Royal Icing as directed. Outline and fill each cooled cookie with white icing, leaving the polar bear's sweater area unfilled. To make a polar bear nose, pipe a mound of stiff icing onto the lower half of the face and let set until almost dry, then press on a mini brown M&M. Pipe on faces, then decorate sweaters, scarves and hats as desired using tinted icing.

MAKE IT A PARTY

Bake up a batch, set out icing and sprinkles and let guests compete to see who can come up with the best ugly sweater design.

WATCH THE OVEN

Smaller cookies take less time to bake than bigger ones. Remove smaller cookies when they are light golden brown around the edges, then return the bigger ones to the oven.

1. Prepare Classic Sugar Cookie Dough as directed. Working with 1 portion at a time (keeping the other portions wrapped in plastic), add a couple drops of green food coloring to dough and mix until fully incorporated. (Tip: Tint slightly darker than you desire; cookies will bake up lighter.) Roll between 2 sheet of parchment paper to ⅛-inch thick. Chill until firm, 30 minutes in refrigerator or 15 minutes in freezer. Repeat with remaining dough.

2. Heat oven to 350°F. Line 2 baking sheets with parchment paper. Using floured graduated round cookie cutters and mini star cookie cutters, cut out cookies and place them on the prepared baking sheets, spacing them 2 inches apart. Reroll, chill and cut the scraps.

3. Bake, rotating the positions of the baking sheets halfway through, until cookies are light golden brown around edges, 10 to 12 minutes. Let cool on baking sheets for 5 minutes before transferring to wire racks to cool completely.

4. Use Royal Icing to "glue" cookies together in a tree shape with a star at top, then dust with confectioners' sugar.

Sugar Cookie Trees

Active Time 30 minutes
Total Time 45 minutes, plus chilling and cooling
Makes 24

1 batch Classic Sugar Cookie Dough (page 82)

Green gel food coloring

Royal icing, for "glue" (page 8)

Confectioners' sugar, for dusting

Alfajores

Active Time 40 minutes | **Total Time** 1 hour, plus cooling | **Makes** 36

1 cup all-purpose flour, plus more for surfaces

1 2/3 cups cornstarch

1 teaspoon baking powder

3/4 teaspoon ground cinnamon

1/4 teaspoon kosher salt

10 tablespoons unsalted butter, at room temperature

1/2 cup sugar

1/2 teaspoon pure vanilla extract

4 large egg yolks

1 16-ounce jar store-bought dulce de leche or about 1 cup Slow-Cooker Dulce de Leche

1. Heat oven to 350°F. Line 2 baking sheets with parchment paper.

2. Into a large bowl, sift flour, cornstarch, baking powder, cinnamon and salt; set aside.

3. Using an electric mixer, beat butter and sugar in a large bowl on medium-high speed until creamy, about 3 minutes. Beat in vanilla, then egg yolks, one at a time. Reduce speed to low, then add flour mixture until just combined.

4. On a lightly floured surface, with a lightly floured rolling pin, roll half the dough to 1/4 inch thick. With a 1 1/2-inch round cutter, cut out rounds. With a small knife or mini offset spatula, place cookies onto the prepared sheets, spacing them 1 inch apart. Reroll scraps once and cut out more rounds.

5. Bake until golden brown on bottom, 12 to 15 minutes. Let cool on baking sheets for 5 minutes before transferring to a wire rack to cool completely. Repeat with remaining rounds.

6. Assemble sandwiches: Place dulce de leche in a piping bag fitted with a star tip, pipe onto half the cookies, then top with remaining cookies. Cookie sandwiches can be stored in airtight containers in the freezer for up to a month.

BONUS RECIPE

Slow-Cooker Dulce de Leche

Transfer **1 can (14 ounces) sweetened condensed milk** to one 1-cup canning jar or three 1/3-cup jars. Stir in **1/8 teaspoon salt** and seal tightly with lid; place in the bowl of a slow cooker (if using a larger jar, lay it down sideways). Cover with water. Place the lid on the slow cooker and cook on Low for 8 hours. Carefully remove the jar from water and wipe dry. Let cool for 1 hour in the refrigerator before opening. Makes about 1 cup.

FESTIVE SWEET

A coffee-shop staple in Argentina, classic alfajores are a caramel-filled delight. For a more traditional take, roll the edges of the caramel filling in shredded sweetened coconut.

Spiced Yule Log Cookies

Active Time 25 minutes | **Total Time** 1 hour, plus chilling and cooling | **Makes** 48

2 ¼ cups all-purpose flour, plus more for dusting

1 teaspoon pumpkin pie spice

¼ teaspoon kosher salt

½ cup (1 stick) unsalted butter, at room temperature

1 cup confectioners' sugar, plus more for dusting

1 large egg, at room temperature, plus 1 large egg white

1 teaspoon pure vanilla extract

Melted white chocolate or buttercream frosting, for decorating

Green gumdrops and red nonpareils, for decorating

1. In a medium bowl, whisk together flour, pumpkin pie spice and salt; set aside.

2. Using an electric mixer, beat butter and sugar in a large bowl until light and creamy, about 3 minutes; scrape down the bowl. Reduce mixer speed to low and beat in 1 egg and vanilla to combine; scrape down the bowl. Gradually add flour mixture, mixing until a stiff dough forms.

3. Divide dough into 8 portions and shape each into a fat log. Wrap each in plastic and refrigerate 1 hour.

4. Heat oven to 350°F. Line 2 baking sheets with parchment paper. On a lightly floured work surface, roll each dough log into an 18-inch rope and cut into 6 logs. Place the logs 1 inch apart on the prepared baking sheets. Cut the ends of each log on a bias, reserving the dough scraps.

5. In a small bowl, beat egg white with 1 teaspoon water. Brush logs with eggwhite wash and attach the reserved dough scraps as "cut stumps" to logs (use 2 stumps per log). Bake until dry and set, 12 to 14 minutes. Slide the parchment onto wire racks and let cool completely.

6. To decorate, lightly dust the logs with confectioners' sugar or lightly frost with melted white chocolate or buttercream. Roll out gumdrops and cut out tiny holly leaves. Attach 2 leaves and 1 red nonpareil to each log with a dab of melted white chocolate. Store in an airtight container at room temperature up to 2 weeks, using wax paper between the layers.

LOG LORE
Inspired by the beloved chocolate log cake, this bite-size spin follows the ancient winter festival tradition of burning (or baking) a log in the holiday season.

Mini Chocolate Chip Sandwiches

Active Time 25 minutes | **Total Time** 35 minutes | **Makes** 25

1½   cups cake flour

½   teaspoon baking powder

½   teaspoon baking soda

½   teaspoon kosher salt

½   cup (1 stick) unsalted butter, at room temperature

¼   cup plus 2 tablespoons granulated sugar

2   tablespoons packed brown sugar

1   large egg

½   teaspoon pure vanilla extract

4   ounces bittersweet chocolate, roughly chopped

4   ounces semisweet chocolate, roughly chopped

Chocolate frosting, for assembly

1. Line 2 large baking sheets with parchment paper. In a medium bowl, sift together cake flour, baking powder, baking soda and salt; set aside.

2. Using an electric mixer, beat butter and sugars in a large bowl on medium speed until light and fluffy, 3 minutes. Reduce speed to low and beat in egg, followed by vanilla. Add flour mixture in 3 additions, mixing until just incorporated. Fold in chocolates.

3. Scoop rounded teaspoonfuls of dough onto the prepared baking sheets, spacing them 2 inches apart. Flatten tops slightly with your hands and freeze for 10 minutes.

4. Heat oven to 350°F. Bake, rotating the positions of the baking sheets after 5 minutes, until cookies are puffed and edges are beginning to turn golden brown, 7 to 8 minutes total. Let cookies cool completely on a cooling rack.

5. Assemble sandwiches: Spread chocolate frosting onto bottom of half the cookies, then top with remaining cookies.

Switch It Up
FESTIVE FLAVOR

Fold store-bought chocolate-hazelnut spread (or make your own, see page 36 for recipe) into chocolate or vanilla frosting.

BONUS RECIPE
Chocolate Frosting

Using an electric mixer, beat **¾ cup unsalted butter** (at room temperature), **2 cups confectioners' sugar**, **1 teaspoon pure vanilla extract** and **pinch kosher salt** in a large bowl on low speed until almost combined, about 2 to 3 minutes. Add **4 ounces semisweet chocolate** (melted and cooled) and **2 ounces unsweetened chocolate** (melted and cooled). Increase speed to high, then beat frosting until light and fluffy, 1 minute. Makes 2 ½ cups.

Home Sweet Home

Begin with our spiced Gingerbread Cookie Dough recipe, then bring your family or friends together to build some magical memories, one house at a time.

Gingerbread Cookie Dough

Active Time 20 minutes | **Total Time** 20 minutes, plus chilling
Makes 36 to 48 (depending on size and shape)

2 ½   cups all-purpose flour

2 ½   teaspoons ground ginger

1 ½   teaspoons ground cinnamon

 ½   teaspoon freshly ground nutmeg

 ½   teaspoon baking soda

 ¼   teaspoon ground cloves

 ¼   teaspoon kosher salt

 ½   cup (1 stick) unsalted butter, at room temperature

 ½   cup firmly packed dark brown sugar

 1   large egg

 ¼   cup molasses (not blackstrap)

1 ½   teaspoons pure vanilla extract

1. In a large bowl, whisk flour, ginger, cinnamon, nutmeg, baking soda, cloves and salt; set aside.

2. Using an electric mixer, beat butter and brown sugar in a large bowl on medium speed until light and fluffy, about 3 minutes. Beat in egg, molasses and vanilla until well blended, scraping the side of the bowl occasionally. Reduce mixer speed to low and gradually beat in flour mixture until just incorporated (dough will be soft).

3. Divide dough into four 1-inch-thick disks. Place each disk in plastic wrap and refrigerate until firm, at least 4 hours and up to 2 days.

Building Basics

Before you break ground, arm your gingerbread construction crew with these tips.

MAKE TWO SETS OF ICING You'll want one with a thicker consistency (think Marshmallow Fluff) for assembling and a thinner one (think buttermilk) for decorating. See pages 8 and 9 for our Royal Icing and Decorators' Icing recipes.

DRY FLAT For intricately piped decor on the walls or roof, decorate the pieces first and let dry completely, at least 8 hours, before raising your house to ensure the establishments stay in place.

BOLSTER SUPPORT Start building the house by securing the corners with thicker icing. Then use canned goods as braces (both inside and out) to keep the walls in place as the icing dries, at least 12 hours.

CONSIDER HOT GLUE Don't plan on eating your house? Save time by gluing the walls and roof together, then use icing for decorating.

Easy Gingerbread House

2 batches Gingerbread Cookie Dough (page 90)

   All-purpose flour, for dusting

1 batch Royal Icing (page 8)

1. Prepare Gingerbread House Dough as directed. Heat oven to 375° F. Line 3 large rimmed baking sheets with parchment paper.

2. Cut out gingerbread house templates (goodhousekeeping.com/gingerbreadstencils). Working with 1 disk at a time, roll dough on a lightly floured work surface to ¼ inch thick. Use a pizza wheel or sharp knife to trace templates, cutting 2 of each shape. (Gather and refrigerate scraps while working with remaining dough; they can be rerolled once.) Transfer gingerbread cutouts to the prepared baking sheets, spacing 1 inch apart and freeze until firm, 15 minutes.

3. In batches, bake cookies 1 tray at a time, rotating the positions of the baking sheets halfway through, until puffed and firm, 25 to 30 minutes. Let cool on the baking sheets 5 minutes, then transfer to wire racks to cool completely. Meanwhile, prepare Royal Icing as directed.

4. Assemble the house: Transfer about 1 ½ cups Royal Icing to a piping bag fitted with a coupler and a ¼-inch round tip. Keep the remaining icing in a bowl, covered with plastic pressed directly on the surface to prevent it from drying out.

5. Pipe a generous bead of icing on the bottom and 1 vertical edge of 1 side of the gingerbread

house and position on a serving platter or board. Holding the piece upright, pipe a bead of icing along the bottom edge of the perpendicular side of the house. Affix the second side of the house to the board, forming a corner with the first piece. Place sturdy cans or glasses around the gingerbread walls to stabilize while icing dries. Pipe a generous bead of icing on the inside corner and bottom edge of both pieces.

6. Repeat with remaining 2 sides of the house. Let sit undisturbed in a cool, dry place until icing sets, at least 4 hours and preferably overnight.

7. Pipe a generous bead of icing along rooflines of the house. Affix roof pieces, using tall glasses to hold them in place while icing dries, 4 hours to overnight. Remove glasses when icing has set. Decorate house as desired.

▲
SNOWY SCENE
Spread icing across the display surface, then sprinkle shredded coco-nut "snow" over top and press down gently to help it stick.

MAKE AHEAD
Baked walls and roof pieces can be prepped in advance and stored in a cool, dry place for up to 1 week before assembling.

Add Curb Appeal

Raid your pantry and the candy aisle for some colorful and creative ways to make a classic gingerbread house a home.

▲ **JOLLY GREEN WREATH**
Slice gumdrops, fan them out into a circle (with slices overlapping) and "glue" them together with Royal Icing.

▲ **WINDOWS AND DOORS**
Break graham crackers into different sizes and shapes and attach to the walls with royal icing.

◀ **STAINED GLASS WINDOWS**
Heat oven to 350°F and bake crushed hard candies in a greased cookie cutter until melted. Let cool completely, pop out of the molds and "glue" to the walls.

▲ **SWEET ENTRY**
Pave a path by attaching chocolate rocks and candy pebbles with Royal Icing.

RAVISHING ROOF
To make shingles, overlap pieces of red sour belts with Royal Icing. Or use sliced almonds to mimic a cedar roof.

STONE CHIMNEY
Coat with Royal Icing and add speckled white jelly beans. Let set before attaching to the house.

LOG WALLS
Use Royal Icing to attach long Tootsie Rolls to the sides of the house, cutting to fit as needed.

Gingerbread People S'mores

Active Time 1 hour 10 minutes | **Total Time** 2 hours 45 minutes | **Makes** 23

1 batch Gingerbread Cookie Dough (page 90)

1 cup bittersweet chocolate chips

1 8-ounce package cream cheese

1 cup marshmallow cream

   Large red nonpareils or red mini candies, for decorating

1. Make Gingerbread Cookie Dough as directed. Roll each disk of cookie dough between 2 sheets of parchment paper to ⅛ inch thick. Refrigerate until firm, about 30 minutes.

2. Heat oven to 350°F. Line 2 baking sheets with parchment paper. Using floured 3 ½-inch gingerbread man cutters, cut out cookies from dough. Place on the prepared sheets, spacing them 1 inch apart. Reroll, chill and cut scraps.

3. Bake, rotating the positions of the baking sheets halfway through, until cookies start to turn golden brown around edges, 10 to 12 minutes. Let cool on the baking sheets for 3 minutes before transferring to a wire rack to cool completely.

4. Meanwhile, in a small bowl, microwave chocolate chips in 20-second intervals, stirring in between, until melted and smooth. Spread 1 teaspoon melted chocolate onto the flat side of half the cookies. Place cookies, chocolate-side up, onto the baking sheet and refrigerate until just set, about 10 minutes.

5. Meanwhile, using an electric mixer, beat cream cheese and marshmallow cream in a large bowl until fluffy, about 2 minutes. Spread 1 rounded teaspoon marshmallow filling onto the flat side of the remaining cookies. Sandwich with chocolate-sided cookies and refrigerate until set, about 20 minutes.

6. Transfer remaining marshmallow filling to a piping bag fitted with a writing tip (or a resealable plastic bag; snip off a corner). Decorate as desired with filling and red nonpareils.

PRACTICE PATIENCE

Waiting for the icing to set can take a while. Cookie size, thickness of the icing, temperature and humidity in your kitchen all play a role in how long it takes.

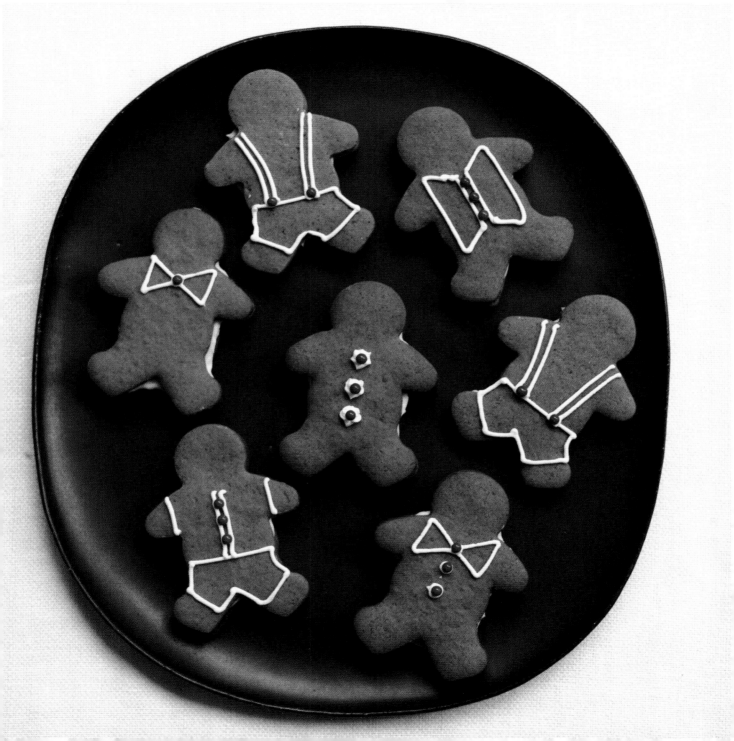

Gingerbread Sandwich Cookies

Active Time 30 minutes | **Total Time** 1 hour | **Makes** 24

FOR THE COOKIES

2 ½   cups all-purpose flour

2 ½   teaspoons ground ginger

1 ½   teaspoons ground cinnamon

½   teaspoon freshly grated nutmeg

½   teaspoon baking soda

¼   teaspoon ground cloves

¼   teaspoon kosher salt

½   cup (1 stick) unsalted butter, at room temperature

½   cup firmly packed dark brown sugar

1   large egg

¼   cup molasses

1 ½   teaspoons pure vanilla extract

Royal Icing (page 8)

Sanding sugar and white pearl dragées, for decorating

FOR THE FROSTING

½   cup (1 stick) unsalted butter, at room temperature

⅓   cup confectioners' sugar

Kosher salt

4   ounces milk chocolate, melted and cooled to room temperature

1. Make the cookies: In a large bowl, whisk together flour, ginger, cinnamon, nutmeg, baking soda, cloves and salt; set aside.

2. Using an electric mixer, beat butter and brown sugar in another large bowl on high speed until light and fluffy, 4 to 6 minutes. Beat in egg, molasses and vanilla. Reduce speed to low and gradually add flour mixture, mixing until just incorporated (dough will be soft).

3. Shape dough into 3 disks and roll each between 2 sheets of parchment paper to ⅛ inch thick. Chill until firm, 30 minutes in the refrigerator or 15 minutes in the freezer.

4. Heat oven to 350°F. Line 2 baking sheets with parchment paper. Using floured cookie cutters, cut out cookies. Place onto the prepared sheets, spacing them 2 inches apart.

5. Bake, rotating the positions of the baking sheets halfway through, until light golden brown around edges, 10 to 12 minutes. Let cool on baking sheets for 5 minutes before transferring to a cooling rack to cool completely.

6. Meanwhile, make chocolate frosting: Using an electric mixer, beat butter, sugar and a pinch of salt in a large bowl on medium speed until light and fluffy, 2 minutes. Reduce speed to low and add melted chocolate, beating to combine.

7. Prepare the Royal Icing. Decorate half the cookies with icing, sanding sugar and dragées as desired. Spread chocolate frosting onto remaining cookie halves and sandwich with decorated halves.

Peanut Butter & Candy Bar Thumbprints

Active Time 45 minutes | **Total Time** 1 hour 30 minutes, including cooling | **Makes** 36

1 ½ cups all-purpose flour

¾ teaspoon baking soda

½ teaspoon baking powder

½ teaspoon kosher salt

½ cup (1 stick) unsalted butter, at room temperature

¾ cup creamy peanut butter

⅓ cup granulated sugar

⅓ cup packed light brown sugar

1 large egg

1 teaspoon pure vanilla extract

½ cup sanding sugar

36 miniature chocolate candy bars, unwrapped

1. Heat oven to 375°F. Line 2 baking sheets with parchment paper. In a medium bowl, whisk together flour, baking soda, baking powder and salt; set aside.

2. Using an electric mixer, beat butter, peanut butter, granulated sugar and brown sugar in a large bowl on medium speed until light and creamy, 1 to 2 minutes. Beat in egg and then vanilla. Reduce speed to low and gradually add flour mixture, mixing until just combined.

3. Place sanding sugar in a small bowl. Scoop rounded tablespoonfuls of dough and drop them into sanding sugar, rolling to coat completely; transfer to the prepared sheets, spacing them 2 inches apart. Press thumb gently into center of each cookie to indent.

4. Bake, in batches, until bottoms are lightly browned, 8 to 10 minutes. Immediately press a candy bar into center of each cookie. Let cool on baking sheets on cooling racks for 10 minutes. Transfer cookies to wire racks to cool completely.

Ginger & Cream Sandwich Bites

Active Time 30 minutes
Total Time 2 hours, plus chilling and cooling
Makes 80

FOR THE COOKIES

2 ¾ cups all-purpose flour
1 teaspoon baking powder
1 teaspoon baking soda
¼ teaspoon kosher salt
¾ cup (1 ½ sticks) unsalted butter, at room temperature
1 ½ cups sugar
1 large egg
¼ cup molasses
1 tablespoon grated peeled fresh ginger

FOR THE FILLING

½ cup (1 stick) unsalted butter, at room temperature
1 teaspoon orange zest
2 cups confectioners' sugar, sifted
1 tablespoon heavy cream

1. Prepare the cookies: In a medium bowl, whisk together flour, baking powder, baking soda and salt; set aside.

2. Using an electric mixer, beat butter and 1 cup sugar in a large bowl on medium speed until light and fluffy, about 3 minutes. Beat in egg, molasses and ginger. Reduce speed to low and gradually add flour mixture, mixing until just incorporated (dough will be soft). Cover and refrigerate until firm enough to handle, about 1 hour.

3. Heat oven to 350°F. Line 2 large baking sheets with parchment paper. Place remaining ½ cup sugar in a small bowl. Working with one baking sheet at a time and keeping dough covered, roll ½ teaspoon dough into a ball and then roll in sugar to coat. Place balls onto the prepared sheet, spacing them 1 inch apart. Freeze until firm, about 15 minutes. Repeat with remaining dough.

4. Bake until cookies are puffed and set, 8 to 10 minutes, rotating the positions of the baking sheets halfway through. Let cool on baking sheets for 2 minutes, then slide parchment paper with cookies onto a cooling rack to cool completely.

5. Meanwhile, make the filling: Using an electric mixer, beat butter in a large bowl on medium speed until creamy, 2 minutes. Add orange zest. Reduce speed to low and gradually add confectioners' sugar, then beat in heavy cream.

6. Once cookies are cool, assemble sandwiches: Spread a small amount of filling onto half the cookies, then top with remaining cookies.

Chocolate Mittens

Active Time 2 hours 40 minutes | **Total Time** 3 hours 50 minutes | **Makes** 32 (depending on size and shape)

- 2 cups all-purpose flour
- ¼ cup unsweetened cocoa, plus more for dusting
- ¼ cup unsweetened black cocoa
- ½ teaspoon baking soda
- ¼ teaspoon kosher salt
- ¾ cup (1 ½ sticks) unsalted butter, at room temperature
- ¾ cup granulated sugar
- 1 large egg
- 2 teaspoons pure vanilla extract
- 1 batch Royal Icing (page 8)

   Red, green, cornflower blue and teal gel food coloring

   White, green and blue sanding sugar, for decorating

1. In a medium bowl, whisk together flour, cocoas, baking soda and salt; set aside.

2. Using an electric mixer, beat butter and sugar in a large bowl on medium-high speed until fluffy, about 3 minutes. Beat in egg, then vanilla. Reduce speed to low and gradually add flour mixture until incorporated.

3. Shape dough into 2 disks and roll each between 2 sheets of parchment paper to ⅛ to ¼ inch thick. Chill until firm, 30 minutes in the refrigerator or 15 minutes in the freezer.

4. Heat oven to 350°F. Line 2 baking sheets with parchment paper. Using cocoa-dusted cutters, cut out cookies. If using as ornaments, use a straw to poke a small hole on one side of each cuff. Place on the prepared sheets, spacing them 2 inches apart. Reroll, chill and cut the scraps.

5. Bake, rotating the positions of the baking sheets halfway through, until cookies are light golden brown around edges, 10 to 12 minutes. Let cool on baking sheets for 5 minutes before transferring to a wire rack to cool completely.

6. Meanwhile, prepare the Royal Icing. Divide icing among 4 bowls; tint 3 bowls with gel food coloring as desired. Add water, 1 teaspoon at a time, to thin all icing to the consistency of marshmallow cream. Transfer ⅓ cup of each color icing to piping bags fitted with writing tips. Slightly thin remaining icing in each bowl with 1 teaspoon water. Place thinned icing in separate resealable plastic bags and snip off the corners. (You should now have 4 piping bags with thick icing and 4 resealable bags with thinner icing.)

7. To decorate, start with the cuffs. Working with one mitten at a time, use thicker icing to pipe the cuff outline. Squirt some thinner icing of the same color inside the outline; use a brush to spread icing within the border. While icing is wet, sprinkle it with sanding sugar; let set. Repeat with remaining mittens.

8. Working with one mitten at a time, use the same method of piping borders with thicker icing and filling in with thinner icing. While icing is wet, pipe lines or dots onto each mitten using different colors of thinner icing. With a toothpick, pull icing through or around to create patterns. Let cookies dry completely, about 1 hour. Thread with ribbon if desired.

FLAVOR MEETS FASHION

Too pretty to eat? String the "mittens" with ribbon and use them as ornaments.

Gingerbread Wands

Active Time 30 minutes
Total Time 45 minutes, plus cooling
Makes 84

½	cup granulated sugar
½	cup molasses (not blackstrap)
1	tablespoon pumpkin pie spice
¼	teaspoon freshly ground black pepper
2	teaspoons baking soda
½	cup (1 stick) unsalted butter, melted
1	large egg
3½	cups all-purpose flour, plus more for dusting
1	large egg white, beaten
	Colored decorating sugar, edible glitter and sprinkles, for decorating

1. Heat oven to 325°F. In a 4-quart saucepan, combine granulated sugar, molasses, pumpkin pie spice and black pepper; bring to a boil, stirring occasionally. Remove from heat; stir in baking soda, then butter. With a fork, stir in egg, then flour until combined.

2. Line a large baking sheet with parchment paper. On a lightly floured work surface, knead dough until smooth; divide in half. Wrap 1 piece of dough in plastic and set aside. With a lightly floured rolling pin, roll remaining half of dough into 12-inch by 8-inch rectangle (it should be about scant ¼-inch thick). With a pizza cutter, cut dough into ¼-inch-wide, 8-inch-long strips. Transfer to the prepared baking sheet, spacing about 1 inch apart.

3. Lightly brush strips with egg white and sprinkle with desired decorations. Bake until set, 12 to 15 minutes. Cool on the baking sheet on a wire rack. Meanwhile, repeat rolling, cutting and decorating with remaining dough. Cookies can be stored in airtight containers at room temperature for up to 2 weeks.

Black Forest Cookies

Active Time 35 minutes | **Total Time** 1 hour 10 minutes, plus cooling | **Makes** 16

FOR THE COOKIES

1	cup all-purpose flour
1/3	cup unsweetened cocoa powder
1/2	teaspoon baking soda
1/4	teaspoon kosher salt
1/2	cup (1 stick) unsalted butter, cut into tablespoons
2	ounces dark chocolate (82%), finely chopped
1/2	cup packed dark brown sugar
1/4	cup granulated sugar
1	large egg, at room temperature
1	teaspoon pure vanilla extract

FOR THE TOPPINGS

1/2	cup brandy, plus splash for whipped cream
2	tablespoons granulated sugar
1	teaspoon cornstarch
1	cup jarred sour cherries, drained
1	cup cold heavy cream
4	teaspoons confectioners' sugar
1/2	teaspoon pure vanilla extract
	Shaved dark chocolate, for sprinkling

1. Make dough: In a medium bowl, whisk together flour, cocoa powder, baking soda and salt; set aside.

2. In a medium saucepan, bring 2 inches of water to a simmer. In a heatproof bowl, combine butter and chocolate, place over (but not in) simmering water and gently melt butter and chocolate together. Remove from heat and whisk in brown and granulated sugars until smooth. Beat in egg, then vanilla. Fold in flour mixture until just incorporated. Cover the bowl and refrigerate until firm, about 30 minutes.

3. Meanwhile, make brandied cherries: In a small saucepan, combine brandy, granulated sugar and cornstarch. Simmer until thickened to consistency of honey, about 3 minutes. Fold in cherries and let mixture cool completely.

4. Make whipped cream: In a large bowl, using an electric mixer with a whisk attachment, beat cream, confectioners' sugar, vanilla and splash of brandy on medium-high until stiff peaks form. Cover the bowl and refrigerate until ready to assemble cookies.

5. Bake cookies: Heat oven to 350°F. Line 2 baking sheets with parchment paper. Roll dough into 16 balls (2 tablespoons each) and divide between the prepared baking sheets, spacing 3 inches apart.

6. Bake, rotating the positions of the baking sheets halfway through, until cookies are just set around the edges and cracks appear on surface, 8 to 10 minutes. Let cookies cool on the baking sheets 5 minutes, then transfer to a wire rack to cool completely.

7. Just before serving, transfer whipped cream to a piping bag fitted with a large star tip and pipe onto cookies; top each with brandied cherry and sprinkle with shaved chocolate.

CHERRY ON TOP

While fresh cherries are a summer staple, jarred ones are gems for the holidays. Pick the sour variety, which has less added sugar than the maraschino kind.

Strawberry Pinwheels

Active Time 45 minutes
Total Time 1 hour 5 minutes, plus chilling and cooling
Makes 35 to 40

2 ¾ cups all-purpose flour

½ teaspoon baking powder

¼ teaspoon kosher salt

1 cup (2 sticks) unsalted butter, at room temperature

¾ cup sugar

1 large egg

1 ½ teaspoons pure vanilla extract

½ ounce freeze-dried strawberries, finely ground in mini food processor and sifted to yield 3 tablespoons

¼ teaspoon red gel food coloring

1. In a large bowl, whisk together flour, baking powder and salt; set aside.

2. Using an electric mixer, beat butter and sugar in a large bowl on medium speed, scraping bowl halfway through, until light and fluffy, about 3 minutes. Beat in egg, then vanilla, scraping the bowl as needed. Reduce mixer speed to low and gradually add flour mixture until just incorporated.

3. Transfer ⅓ of dough to a piece of parchment. To remaining dough, add strawberry powder and food coloring; beat on medium-low until evenly colored. Shape each piece of dough into a rectangle. Between 2 sheets of parchment, roll plain dough into a 10- by 12-inch rectangle. Repeat with strawberry dough.

4. Stack plain dough on strawberry dough (with parchment intact) on a baking sheet; refrigerate 20 minutes. Remove top parchment piece from each. Using the parchment, invert plain dough onto strawberry dough to line up the edges.

5. Peel off the top parchment and discard. Starting from the long side, tightly roll stacked doughs together into 1 log, lifting the bottom piece of parchment to help roll (if dough is stiff, let it warm up). Lightly pinch the seam to seal. Wrap log in plastic and freeze until dough is firm enough to slice, 1 to 2 hours. (Dough can be frozen up to 3 months. Let thaw slightly at room temp to ease slicing; cookies may need an extra 1 to 2 minutes baking.)

6. Heat oven to 350°F. Line 2 baking sheets with parchment. Slice log 1/4-inch thick and place on the prepared baking sheets, 1 inch apart. Bake, rotating the positions of the baking sheets halfway through, until tops of cookies look dry, 15 to 18 minutes. Let cool on the baking sheets 5 minutes, then transfer to wire racks to cool completely.

**CAKE,
MEET COOKIE**

Cake flour gives these
slice-inspired cookies
a softer and fluffier
texture than all-purpose
flour. Make your own:
Sift together ¾ cups
all-purpose flour with
¼ cup cornstarch
(yields 2 cups).

Stuffed Red Velvet Cookies

Active Time 25 minutes | **Total Time** 50 minutes, plus freezing and cooling | **Makes** 26 to 28

FOR THE FILLING

6	ounces cold cream cheese
3	tablespoons confectioners' sugar
1	teaspoon cake flour
	Pinch kosher salt
¼	teaspoon pure vanilla extract

FOR THE COOKIES

1 ⅓	cups cake flour
¼	cup unsweetened cocoa powder
¾	teaspoon baking powder
½	teaspoon kosher salt
½	cup (1 stick) unsalted butter, at room temperature
½	cup granulated sugar
½	cup light brown sugar
2	teaspoons pure vanilla extract
1	large egg, at room temperature
2	teaspoons red gel food coloring
¼	cup granulated sugar, for rolling

1. Make filling: Line a baking sheet with parchment paper. In a small bowl, using a fork or pastry blender, combine cream cheese with confectioners' sugar, flour, salt and vanilla until just incorporated. Freeze mixture until firm enough to roll into balls, 10 to 15 minutes. When firm, roll into teaspoon-size balls and place on the prepared baking sheet. Freeze until solid, at least 1½ hours.

2. Make cookies: Line a baking sheet with parchment paper. In a medium bowl, whisk together flour, cocoa powder, baking powder and salt; set aside. Using an electric mixer fitted with paddle attachment, cream butter, sugars and vanilla in a large bowl on medium, 3 minutes, scraping down the bowl as necessary. Beat in egg and food coloring. Gradually add flour mixture until just incorporated, scraping the bowl as necessary. Refrigerate until slightly firm, 15 to 20 minutes.

3. When balls are firm and dough is slightly firm but still pliable, form 1-tablespoon balls of red velvet dough. Press a deep thumbprint into each dough ball and insert a ball of filling; pinch dough around filling to fully enclose it and gently roll with your hands to form an even sphere. Place on a prepared baking sheet and refrigerate until firm, at least 10 minutes (or refrigerate in an airtight container up to 1 week).

4. Heat oven to 350°F. Line another baking sheet with parchment paper. Meanwhile, roll cookies: Roll balls in granulated sugar and place on the prepared baking sheets, spacing 2 inches apart. Bake, rotating the positions of the baking sheets halfway through, until firm around edges, 12 to 14 minutes. Slide the parchment with cookies on a wire rack and let cool at least 15 minutes before serving. Cookies are best baked and eaten on the same day.

CHOCOLATE-
COVERED
PRETZELS
page 121

CHAPTER 5

NOT-QUITE COOKIES

These treats are anything but cookie-cutter. From White Peppermint Bark to Eggnog Truffles and Cranberry Swirl Cheesecake Bars, these goodies may not be cookies, but they're guaranteed crowd-pleasers at any holiday celebration.

Layered Fudge

Active Time 30 minutes | **Total Time** 30 minutes, plus chilling | **Makes** 32

FOR THE NUT BUTTER FUDGE

Nonstick cooking spray, for the pan

1 ¾ cups sugar

⅓ cup whole milk

4 tablespoons unsalted butter

1 cup creamy nut butter

1½ teaspoons pure vanilla extract

¼ teaspoon kosher salt

FOR THE CHOCOLATE NUT BUTTER FUDGE

⅔ cup semisweet chocolate chips

¾ cup sugar

3 tablespoons whole milk

2 tablespoons unsalted butter

½ cup creamy nut butter

½ teaspoon pure vanilla extract

⅛ teaspoon kosher salt

Flaky salt, for sprinkling

1. Lightly coat an 8-inch square baking pan with cooking spray and line with parchment paper, leaving a 2-inch overhang on two opposite sides.

2. Make nut butter fudge: In a medium saucepan, combine sugar, milk and butter. Cook on medium, stirring to melt butter and dissolve sugar. Bring to a boil, stirring frequently, about 3 minutes. Remove from heat and stir in nut butter, vanilla and salt until thoroughly combined. Spread mixture in the prepared pan and, using a small offset spatula, smooth into an even layer. Set aside.

3. Make chocolate nut butter fudge: In a medium bowl, microwave chocolate in 20-second intervals, stirring in between, until melted and smooth, about 1 minute total. In a medium saucepan, combine sugar, milk and butter. Cook on medium, stirring to melt butter and dissolve sugar. Bring mixture to a boil, stirring frequently, 1 ½ minutes. Remove from heat and stir in melted chocolate, nut butter, vanilla and salt until combined.

4. Working quickly, transfer mounds of chocolate fudge on top of nut butter fudge and, using a small offset spatula, pat and spread into an even, smooth layer (fudge will stiffen but will smooth out with some coaxing). Sprinkle top with flaky salt. Cover the pan with plastic wrap and refrigerate until fudge is firm, at least 2 hours.

5. Use the overhang to lift out fudge and transfer to a cutting board. Cut into bars and package as desired. Store at room temperature in an airtight container for up to 1 week or in refrigerator for up to 2 weeks.

WRAP IT UP
This easy, no-bake treat is perfect for parties and gift giving. Roll individual pieces in parchment paper and tie with ribbon.

White Chocolate & Peppermint Blondies

Active Time 25 minutes | **Total Time** 3 hours | **Makes** 18

Nonstick cooking spray, for the pan

¾ cup (1 ½ sticks) unsalted butter, melted

¾ cup granulated sugar

⅔ cup packed light brown sugar

3 large eggs, at room temperature

¼ teaspoon pure peppermint extract

2 teaspoons pure vanilla extract

2 ⅔ cups all-purpose flour

¾ teaspoon baking powder

¼ teaspoon kosher salt

1 ½ cups coarsely chopped white chocolate

1 16-ounce package cream cheese

1 cup confectioners' sugar

¾ cup peppermints, crushed

1. Heat oven to 325°F. Lightly coat a 9- by 13-inch baking pan with nonstick cooking spray. Line pan with parchment paper, leaving a 2-inch overhang on the two long sides; spray paper.

2. In a medium bowl, whisk together butter, granulated sugar, brown sugar, eggs, peppermint extract and 1 teaspoon vanilla to combine. In another bowl, whisk together flour, baking powder and salt. Stir flour mixture into butter mixture to combine. Stir in chocolate. Spread batter in the prepared pan.

3. Bake until golden brown and a wooden pick inserted into the center comes out clean, 30 to 35 minutes. Let cool completely in the pan.

4. Using an electric mixer, beat cream cheese and confectioners' sugar in a large bowl on medium speed until light and fluffy, 1 to 2 minutes. Beat in remaining 1 teaspoon vanilla. Spread frosting on blondies; sprinkle with peppermints. Freeze until frosting is set, 30 minutes. Use overhangs to transfer to a cutting board and cut into squares.

Eggnog Truffles

Active Time 45 minutes
Total Time 45 minutes, plus chilling
Makes 45

- ½ cup heavy cream
- 2 ounces cream cheese, at room temperature
- 1 tablespoon dark rum
- 24 ounces white chocolate, chopped and divided
- 2 cups gingersnap cookie crumbs, from about 44 cookies (we used Anna's Ginger Thins)

  Freshly grated nutmeg and cinnamon, for topping

1. In a medium saucepan, cook cream, cream cheese and rum on medium-low stirring often, until cream cheese melts and mixture is hot to the touch (do not boil).

2. Remove from heat, add 12 ounces chocolate and stir until completely melted. Fold in crushed cookies. Transfer mixture to a bowl, cover and refrigerate until firm, at least 2 hours.

3. Line a large rimmed baking sheet with parchment paper. Use a small spoon to scoop truffle mixture into tablespoon-size balls, carefully rolling between your hands. Place on the prepared baking sheet and freeze until very cold and firm, at least 30 minutes.

4. In a medium bowl, microwave remaining 12 ounces chocolate in 20-second intervals, stirring in between, until melted and smooth. Dip the balls in chocolate, tapping off the excess and transfer back to the baking sheet. Sprinkle with the nutmeg and cinnamon and refrigerate until ready to serve.

Cherry-Ginger Hermit Squares

Active Time 20 minutes | **Total Time** 50 minutes, plus cooling | **Makes** 32

Nonstick cooking spray, for the pan

3 cups all-purpose flour

1 teaspoon baking soda

1 teaspoon cinnamon

1/2 teaspoon kosher salt

3/4 cup (1 1/2 sticks) unsalted butter, at room temperature

1 cup granulated sugar

1/2 cup molasses

1/2 cup dried cherries, chopped

1/3 cup candied ginger, chopped, plus sliced candied ginger, for serving

1/2 cup confectioners' sugar

1 teaspoon orange zest, plus more for serving

2 tablespoons fresh orange juice (from 1/2 small orange)

1. Heat oven to 350°F. Lightly coat a 9- by 13-inch metal baking pan with nonstick cooking spray. Line with parchment paper, leaving a 2-inch overhang on the two long sides; spray paper.

2. In a medium bowl, whisk together flour, baking soda, cinnamon and salt until combined; set aside.

3. Using an electric mixer, beat butter and sugar in a large bowl on high speed until light and fluffy, about 3 minutes. Add molasses and mix until fully incorporated. Reduce speed to low and gradually add flour mixture, beating until a soft dough forms. Fold in cherries and candied ginger.

4. Using your hands, press dough evenly into the prepared pan. Bake until puffed and just barely pulling away from sides, 25 to 30 minutes (it will keep cooking in the pan). Let cool completely in the pan.

5. In a medium bowl, whisk together confectioners' sugar, orange zest and juice until smooth. Drizzle glaze over cooled bars, then sprinkle with zest and sliced candied ginger if desired.

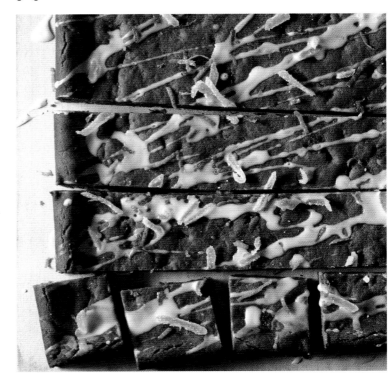

Palmiers

Active Time 35 minutes
Total Time 1 hour 55 minutes
Makes 32

1½ cups (3 sticks) cold unsalted butter, cut into small pieces

3 cups all-purpose flour, plus more for dusting

¾ cup sour cream

1 cup sugar, divided

1. In a large bowl, with a pastry blender or 2 knives used scissor-fashion, cut butter into flour until mixture resembles coarse crumbs. Stir in sour cream. Transfer mixture to a lightly floured work surface and knead until dough holds together. Flatten dough into an 8- by 6-inch rectangle. Place in plastic wrap and refrigerate until firm enough to roll, at least 2 ½ hours or overnight.

2. Heat oven to 400°F. Divide dough in half. Wrap half and return to refrigerator. Sprinkle ½ cup sugar evenly over work surface.

3. Roll remaining half of dough on the sugared work surface into a 14-inch square. Using the side of your hand, make an indentation along the center of dough. Starting from one side, tightly roll dough to indentation. Roll up other side of dough until it meets the first roll. Refrigerate 2 hours or up to 3 days, or freeze up to 3 weeks. Repeat with remaining piece of dough and remaining ½ cup sugar.

4. With a serrated knife, cut 1 roll crosswise into ¼-inch-thick slices. (Return roll to refrigerator if it becomes too soft to slice.) Place slices, 2 inches apart, on 2 large ungreased baking sheets.

5. Bake 10 minutes. With wide metal spatula, carefully turn cookies over. Rotate the positions of the baking sheets and bake until sugar has caramelized and cookies are deep golden brown, about 5 minutes longer. Let cool on the baking sheets 1 minute, then transfer to wire racks to cool completely. Repeat with remaining dough. Store in an airtight container between layers of wax paper up to 1 week or freeze up to 3 months.

Rolling and Cutting Palmiers

These intricate treats only look complicated.

1

Roll up the dough from each side of a 14-inch square to meet at a mark in the center. Incorporate as much sugar as possible as you roll.

2

Cut shaped dough crosswise into ¼-inch-thick slices with a serrated knife. If the dough seems soft, chill it before cutting.

SHORTCUT SWEET

These flaky French pastries (sometimes called elephant ears) can also be made using store-bought puff pastry.

Cranberry Swirl Cheesecake Bars

Active Time 30 minutes
Total Time 1 hour 40 minutes
Makes 12

- ½ cup cranberries (thawed if frozen)
- ½ cup frozen raspberries, thawed
- 1 teaspoon freshly grated orange zest, plus ¼ cup orange juice
- 1 cup granulated sugar
- 4 tablespoons (½ stick) unsalted butter, melted, plus more for the pan
- 1 9-ounce package chocolate wafer cookies
- 3 8-ounce packages cream cheese, at room temperature
- ¾ cup sour cream
- 2 tablespoons all-purpose flour
- 2 teaspoons pure vanilla extract
- 3 large eggs

1. In a medium saucepan, combine cranberries, raspberries, orange zest, juice and ¼ cup sugar. Simmer, stirring occasionally, until cranberries burst and sauce thickens, 5 to 7 minutes. Transfer mixture to a food processor and puree until smooth. Strain into a medium bowl; let cool for 10 minutes, then refrigerate until ready to use.

2. Heat oven to 375°F. Grease a 9- by 13-inch baking pan. In a clean food processor, pulse chocolate wafers into fine crumbs. Add melted butter and pulse to incorporate. Press crumb mixture into the bottom and 2 ½ inches up the sides of the pan. Bake until crust is set and fragrant, 10 to 12 minutes. Transfer to a wire rack to cool. Reduce oven temperature to 325°F.

3. While crust is cooling, using an electric mixer, beat together cream cheese, sour cream, flour, vanilla and remaining ¾ cup sugar in a large bowl until smooth. Beat in eggs, one at a time. Transfer ½ cup filling to a bowl; set aside. Pour remaining filling into cooled crust.

4. Whisk reserved filling into cranberry mixture (it will be thin), then transfer to a resealable plastic bag. Snip a tiny corner off the bag and pipe lines lengthwise over batter. Drag a skewer across lines to form a pattern. Bake until cheesecake is just set (center should still wobble slightly), 18 to 20 minutes. Let cool completely, then refrigerate for at least 3 hours before cutting into bars.

Cookie-Stuffed Brownies

Active Time 15 minutes | **Total Time** 1 hour | **Makes** 16

Nonstick cooking spray, for the pan

1	cup (2 sticks) unsalted butter, cut into pieces
1½	cups packed brown sugar
½	cup granulated sugar
½	teaspoon kosher salt
½	cup bittersweet chocolate chips
3	large eggs
2	teaspoons pure vanilla extract
1½	cups unsweetened cocoa powder
¾	cup all-purpose flour
18	chocolate sandwich cookies, roughly chopped

1. Heat oven to 350°F. Lightly coat a 9-inch square baking pan with nonstick cooking spray.

2. In a large bowl, combine butter, sugars and salt, and microwave on High in 30-second intervals, stirring between each, until butter is melted. Whisk until mixture is combined and glossy, then stir in chocolate chips, whisking to melt. Let cool, whisking occasionally, 5 minutes.

3. When butter mixture is cool, whisk in eggs, one at a time, then vanilla. Stir in cocoa and then flour until just combined. Fold in half the chopped sandwich cookies, then transfer batter to the prepared pan. Scatter remaining cookies on top.

4. Bake until set and a wooden pick inserted 2 inches from the center comes out with a few moist crumbs attached, 35 to 45 minutes. Cut into squares.

Kleicha

Active Time 1 hour 5 minutes | **Total Time** 1 hour 55 minutes, plus rising and cooling | **Makes** 22

FOR THE DOUGH

6 to 9	tablespoons warm water (about 120°F)
1 1/2	teaspoons active dry yeast
2	teaspoons honey
1/2	cup (1 stick) unsalted butter, melted and warm
2 1/2	cups all-purpose flour, plus more for rolling
3/4	teaspoon kosher salt
2	teaspoons nigella seed or 1 teaspoon cumin seed, both optional
1	large egg, beaten well
1 1/2	teaspoons sesame seeds

FOR THE FILLING

10	ounces medjool dates, pitted (about 15 large dates)
1/2	teaspoon cinnamon
3/4	teaspoon ground cardamom
2	tablespoons melted extra-virgin coconut oil or safflower oil
1/3	cup boiling water
1/4	teaspoon kosher salt

1. Using an electric mixer, beat together 6 tablespoons warm water, yeast and honey; let stand until mixture starts to foam, 10 minutes. Add butter and then flour, salt and, if using, nigella or cumin seed. Mix on low speed until flour is just incorporated and dough is hydrated but not sticky, adding up to 3 more tablespoons water as necessary.

2. Transfer dough to work surface and knead lightly to form a mass, then return to the bowl. Cover tightly with plastic wrap and let rise in a warm place, 40 minutes.

3. Heat oven to 350°F, and make the date filling: In a food processor, combine filling ingredients and process until a somewhat smooth paste forms. Date mixture should be spreadable. Adjust with a bit more water if necessary. Divide the dough in half and wrap one half in plastic.

4. Dust a large piece of parchment paper with flour. Place dough on top and form into a square. Sprinkle with flour and roll into a 12-inch square, 1/8-to 1/16 inch thick. (Slide a long offset metal spatula underneath to make sure dough can release from parchment.)

5. Dollop half the date mixture onto dough; spread evenly with an offset spatula, bringing mixture fully to the edge closest to you and within an inch of all other edges.

6. Starting with edge closest to you, roll dough tightly into a log and flip seam-side down. Gently press to flatten slightly. Brush surface with beaten egg and then sprinkle half the sesame seeds on top. Using a serrated knife, cut dough on a slight bias into 1-inch-thick rounds.

7. Place slices, seam-side down, upright on a parchment-lined baking sheet, spacing them 3 inches apart. Bake, rotating the positions of the baking sheets halfway through, until golden brown, 20 to 22 minutes. Transfer to a wire rack to let cool. Repeat with remaining dough and filling.

Brown Butter Crispy Rice Treats

Active Time 20 minutes
Total Time 20 minutes
Makes 9

Nonstick cooking spray, for the pan

6   tablespoons (¾ stick) unsalted butter

1   12-ounces bag marshmallows

6   cups crispy rice cereal (we used Rice Krispies)

Flaky sea salt, for topping

1. Line an 8-inch square baking pan with parchment paper, leaving a 2-inch overhang on two opposite sides; coat with nonstick cooking spray.

2. In a large pot, melt butter on medium. Continue to cook, watching carefully, until beginning to brown and smell nutty, 8 to 10 minutes. (Butter will bubble and sizzle.) Remove from heat, add marshmallows and stir until melted and smooth, 3 to 4 minutes. Add cereal and stir until thoroughly coated, 2 minutes.

3. Transfer to the prepared baking pan and press down until level. Sprinkle with flaky sea salt. Cut into 9 squares.

DELIGHTFUL DATE

These traditional Iraqi swirls are made with medjool dates, the softer and plumper variety that are fresh, not dried. Sub in 10 ounces pitted deglet noor dates in a pinch: They're smaller and can sometimes be hard or dry, so for easier blending, soften them first by soaking them in boiling water for 1 to 2 minutes, then draining.

Eggnog Madeleines

Active Time 25 minutes
Total Time 2 hours 45 minutes
Makes 28

- 1 cup cake flour
- 1 teaspoon baking powder
- Pinch ground cloves
- 1 teaspoon ground cinnamon, divided
- 1 teaspoon freshly grated nutmeg, divided
- 2 large eggs
- ½ cup plus ⅓ cup sugar, divided
- 1 tablespoon honey
- 1 teaspoon pure vanilla extract
- ¼ teaspoon kosher salt
- ½ cup (1 stick) unsalted butter, melted, plus more for the pan
- 2 tablespoons eggnog

1. In a large bowl, sift together flour, baking powder, cloves, ½ teaspoon cinnamon and ½ teaspoon nutmeg; set aside.

2. Using an electric mixer, whisk together eggs and ½ cup sugar in a large bowl until thick and pale, 1 to 2 minutes. Whisk in honey, vanilla and salt. Whisk in flour mixture. Whisk in melted butter and eggnog. Cover and refrigerate at least 2 hours or up to 12 hours.

3. In a small bowl, stir together remaining ⅓ cup sugar, ½ teaspoon cinnamon and ½ teaspoon nutmeg; set aside.

4. Heat oven to 375°F. Brush the wells of a madeleine pan (wells should measure 3 ¼ by 2 inches) with melted butter. Spoon or pipe about 1 tablespoon filling into each well. Bake until golden brown and cookies spring back slightly when pressed, 7 to 8 minutes. Invert cookies onto a wire rack. Toss warm cookies, one at a time, in spiced sugar mixture.

EASY OUT
Rapping the pan, or gently banging it on the counter after baking, will help release the soft and spongy treats so you don't dent them with your fingers.

Jammy Walnut Rugelach

Active Time 35 minutes
Total Time 2 hours 50 minutes, plus chilling
Makes 22

- 1 cup all-purpose flour, plus more for dusting
- ¼ teaspoon kosher salt
- ½ cup (1 stick) cold unsalted butter, cut into small pieces
- 4 ounces cold cream cheese, cut into chunks
- ¼ cup sugar
- ½ teaspoon ground cinnamon
  Pinch ground cloves
- ½ cup apricot or raspberry jam, divided
- ½ cup toasted, finely chopped walnuts, divided
- 1 large egg

1. In a food processor, pulse flour and salt to combine. Add butter and cream cheese and pulse until crumbly dough forms that holds together when squeezed.

2. Transfer dough to a work surface, gently knead to form a cohesive mass, then shape into 5- by 4-inch rectangle. Halve crosswise, wrap each rectangle in plastic and refrigerate until firm, 1 ½ to 2 hours.

3. Meanwhile, in a small bowl, combine sugar, cinnamon and cloves. Transfer 1 tablespoon to a small bowl and set aside. Line a baking sheet with parchment paper.

4. Working with 1 dough rectangle (keep other chilled) on a lightly floured work surface, roll out to 12- by 9-inch rectangle, sprinkling the top with flour to prevent sticking. Spread with

¼ cup jam, then sprinkle with ¼ cup walnuts and half of remaining spiced sugar. Starting from 1 longer side, gently roll up dough into a tight log and transfer to the prepared baking sheet. Freeze until completely firm, at least 30 minutes. Repeat with remaining dough, jam, walnuts and spiced sugar.

5. Heat oven to 350°F. Line a second baking sheet with parchment paper. In a small bowl, whisk together egg and 1 teaspoon water. Transfer chilled logs to a cutting board and trim the edges. Using a serrated knife, cut each log into 1-inch pieces (for a total of 22 rugelach). Transfer rugelach, dough-side up, to the prepared baking sheets, spacing 1 ½ inches apart. Freeze 15 minutes.

6. Lightly brush frozen rugelach with egg mixture and sprinkle with reserved tablespoon spiced sugar. Bake until golden brown and jam starts to bubble around the edges, 25 to 30 minutes. Using tongs, immediately transfer rugelach to a wire rack to cool.

KEEP IT COOL

This rich and delicate dough can get soft easily. To prevent sticking, chill the dough when not using it and keep your work surface generously dusted with flour.

Shortcut Sweets

Who says holiday cookies have to be homemade?

WHITE CHOCOLATE-DIPPED MADELEINES

Partially dip **store-bought madeleine cookies** in **melted white chocolate** on a diagonal and transfer to a parchment-lined baking sheet. Sprinkle with **finely chopped cranberries** and **pistachios** and let set.

Melt Chocolate Like a Pro

These two foolproof methods result in smooth and melty chocolate, perfect for dipping and drizzling.

STOVE TOP Place chopped chocolate or chocolate chips in a metal or glass bowl set over (but not in) a saucepan of simmering water and heat, stirring occasionally, until melted and smooth.

MICROWAVE Place chopped chocolate or chocolate chips in a bowl and microwave on high in 20-second increments, stirring in between, until melted and smooth, about 1 minute total.

WHITE PEPPERMINT BARK

Line a large baking sheet with parchment paper. In a small bowl, microwave **1 pound white chocolate** in 20-second intervals, stirring in between, until melted and smooth. Add in **⅛ teaspoon pure peppermint extract**. Spread onto the prepared baking sheet into roughly 8- by 10-inch rectangle shape. Sprinkle with **white chocolate–coated pretzels, puffed-rice cereal, meringue cookie pieces, white and silver sprinkles** and **crushed peppermint candies**. Refrigerate until set, at least 30 minutes and cut into pieces before serving.

CHOCOLATE-DRIZZLED PRETZELS

Dip **large pretzels** fully or halfway in **melted dark, milk, white,** and/or **strawberry chocolate**, tapping off excess, then transfer to a wax paper-lined baking sheet and let set. Drizzle with another color or same chocolate and let set before serving.

No Time to Bake?

Embellish off-the-shelf cookies — no one will know these treats took you less than 10 minutes to make.

DRIZZLE IT Place store-bought **cookies** on a wire rack set over parchment paper or foil. Make a fast glaze (whisk together **1 ¼ cups confectioners' sugar**, **2 tablespoons lemon juice** or water and **1 teaspoon grated lemon zest** (optional) until smooth). Drizzle over cookies and let set.

DIP IT Dunk **cookies** halfway into **melted white** or **bittersweet chocolate**, letting any excess drip off, then transfer to parchment to let set 5 minutes. Sprinkle with **colored sugars** or **nonpareils**.

SANDWICH IT Tint **store-bought frosting** with **gel food coloring**. Sandwich the frosting between two matching **store-bought cookies** and sprinkle the outside of the frosting with **shredded coconut** or **chopped nuts** such as pistachios or walnuts.

JAM PIE BITES

Line a baking sheet with parchment paper. Gently unroll **1 refrigerated rolled pie crust (half of 14.1-ounce package)**, cut into nine 2 ½-inch squares and transfer to the prepared baking sheet. In a small bowl, gently beat **1 large egg** and **1 teaspoon milk** to make egg wash. Divide **1/4 cup jam (drained of liquid)** among each square, about 1 teaspoon each. Pull 1 corner toward center, covering some jam; brush opposite corner with egg wash; then fold over, pressing gently to adhere. Brush the overlapping corner with egg wash (do not egg-wash rest of dough). Sprinkle **sugar** over egg wash and space evenly on the prepared sheet. Freeze 20 minutes. Heat oven to 400ºF. Bake until pastry is golden brown and jam is bubbling, 17 to 20 minutes. Let cool on the baking sheet 1 minute, then transfer to a wire rack to cool completely. Makes 9.

BONUS RECIPE

10-Minute Berry Jam

In a large bowl, mash **2 cups berries** and **1/3 cup sugar**. Microwave, uncovered, for 10 minutes, stirring once. Let cool completely. Makes 3/4 cup.

NO-BAKE WAFFLE DIPPERS

Dip **store-bought waffle cookies** halfway in **melted bittersweet chocolate** and transfer to a parchment-lined baking sheet. Sprinkle with **toasted shredded coconut** while wet and let set.

FOR YOU

CHOCOLATE
WALNUT
COOKIES
page 132

CHAPTER 6

VEGAN & GLUTEN-FREE FAVORITES

These tested-'til-perfect treats, like vegan truffles made with coconut milk or flourless peanut butter cookies, are crafted with creativity so there's something for everyone at the holiday table this year.

Blood Orange & Olive Oil Shortbread

Active Time 15 minutes
Total Time 30 minutes, plus cooling
Makes 48

3	cups all-purpose flour
½	teaspoon kosher salt
2 ¼	cups confectioners' sugar
1	cup extra virgin olive oil
2	teaspoons pure vanilla extract
2	tablespoons blood orange juice

1. Heat oven to 350°F. In a large bowl, whisk together flour, salt and 1 cup confectioners' sugar. Add oil and vanilla, and mix to combine.

2. Roll dough between 2 pieces of parchment paper to ¼ inch thick. Slide rolled dough onto a baking sheet, remove top piece of parchment and bake until edges are light golden brown, about 15 minutes. While still warm on the baking sheet, cut shortbread into 1- by 2-inch rectangles, but do not move or handle. Let cool completely, about 30 minutes.

3. In a small bowl, whisk together blood orange juice and remaining 1 ¼ cups confectioners' sugar. Dip cooled cookies into glaze diagonally and place on parchment to dry. Store covered at room temperature for up to a week.

BYE-BYE, BUTTER

Using pantry-friendly olive oil in these delicious shortbreads keeps the recipe dairy-free and imparts a sweet and savory flavor to an otherwise buttery bake.

Chocolate Chip Cookies

Active Time 20 minutes | **Total Time** 35 minutes, plus freezing | **Makes** 24

- 2 cups all-purpose flour
- 1 teaspoon baking soda
- ½ teaspoon kosher salt
- 1 cup dairy-free bittersweet chocolate chips
- 1 cup dairy-free semisweet chocolate chips
- ½ cup firmly packed dark brown sugar
- ½ cup granulated sugar
- ½ cup canola oil
- ¼ cup water
- 2 teaspoons pure vanilla extract

1. In a medium bowl, whisk together flour, baking soda and salt. Toss with chocolate chips; set aside.

2. In a second bowl, break up brown sugar, making sure there are no lumps. Add granulated sugar, oil, water and vanilla, and whisk to combine. Add flour mixture and mix until just combined (there should be no streaks of flour).

3. Line 2 baking sheets with parchment paper. Scoop ¼ cupfuls of dough onto the prepared sheets, spacing them 2 inches apart, gently gathering dough together with hands without pressing. (Dough will be crumbly.) Freeze for 30 minutes.

4. Heat oven to 375°F. Bake, rotating the positions of the baking sheets after 6 minutes, until edges are golden brown, 10 to 13 minutes total (cookies will be soft and will continue to cook). Let cool on baking sheets on a cooling rack.

PLANT-BASED CHOCOLATE

Not all chocolate is dairy free. Many bars and most semisweet chips include milk solids, so look for ones labeled "vegan" if you want to keep this recipe 100 percent plant-based.

Oatmeal Chocolate Chip Cookies

Active Time 30 minutes
Total Time 1 hour 15 minutes
Makes 20

1 ½   cups all-purpose flour

1   teaspoon ground cinnamon

1   teaspoon baking soda

½   teaspoon kosher salt

¼   teaspoon freshly grated nutmeg

2   cups old-fashioned rolled oats

2   cups dairy-free bittersweet chocolate chips

½   cup firmly packed dark brown sugar

½   cup granulated sugar

½   cup canola oil

2   teaspoons pure vanilla extract

½   cup water

1. Line 2 baking sheets with parchment paper. In a large bowl, whisk together flour, cinnamon, baking soda, salt and nutmeg. Toss with oats and chocolate chips; set aside.

2. In a second bowl, break up brown sugar, making sure there are no lumps. Add granulated sugar, oil, vanilla and water, and whisk to combine. Add flour mixture and mix until just combined (there should be

no streaks of flour). Scoop 2-inch mounds onto the prepared sheets, spacing them 2 inches apart. Freeze for 30 minutes.

3. Heat oven to 375°F. Bake, rotating the positions of the baking sheets after 6 minutes, until edges are golden brown, 9 to 12 minutes total. Let cool.

OOEY-GOOEY UPGRADE

Chocolate chips are actually created so they don't fully melt. For that perfect gooey texture, sub in chopped chocolate or large chocolate discs instead.

PB & Grape Jamwiches

Active Time 40 minutes
Total Time 1 hour 15 minutes, including cooling
Makes 30

1	cup creamy peanut butter
¾	cup packed light brown sugar
1	large egg
¾	teaspoon baking soda
½	cup peanuts, finely chopped
½	cup Concord grape jam

1. Heat oven to 350°F. Line 2 or 3 large baking sheets with parchment paper. Using an electric mixer, beat peanut butter, brown sugar, egg and baking soda in a large bowl on medium speed until fully incorporated, about 2 minutes.

2. Roll dough into ¾-inch balls (about a level teaspoon each) and coat half the balls with chopped nuts. Place balls onto the prepared sheets, spacing them 2 inches apart.

3. Bake until cookies are puffed and starting to turn light golden brown around edges, 8 to 10 minutes. Let cool on baking sheets for 5 minutes before transferring to a wire rack to cool completely. Repeat with any remaining balls, if necessary.

4. Assemble sandwiches: Spread ½ teaspoon jam onto bottom of each plain cookie, then top with a nut-coated cookie.

White Chocolate Peppermint Patties

Active Time 30 minutes | **Total Time** 1 hour 10 minutes | **Makes** 30

- 4 cup confectioners' sugar
- 4 tablespoons unsalted butter, at room temperature
- ¼ cup heavy cream
- 1½ teaspoons pure peppermint extract
- ½ teaspoon pure vanilla extract
- ½ teaspoon kosher salt
  Nonstick cooking spray, for the wax paper
- 12 ounces white chocolate, chopped
- 2 tablespoons solid coconut oil
  Crushed peppermints, for garnish

1. Line 2 baking sheets with parchment paper. Using an electric mixer, beat confectioners' sugar, butter, cream, peppermint and vanilla extracts and salt in a large bowl on low speed until smooth, 1 to 2 minutes. Roll into 30 balls. Place on the prepared baking sheets and flatten into ¼-inch-thick disks using a greased piece of wax paper. Cover and freeze 30 minutes.

2. In a medium bowl, microwave chocolate and coconut oil in 20-second intervals, stirring in between, until melted and smooth.

3. Place 1 chilled peppermint disk on the tines of a fork and dip into melted chocolate, tapping off excess; return to the baking sheet. Repeat with remaining peppermint disks. Sprinkle tops with crushed peppermints. Chill until set, 15 to 20 minutes. Store, refrigerated, in an airtight container up to 1 week.

Sea-Salted Nut Butter Cups

Active Time 15 minutes | **Total Time** 15 minutes, plus freezing | **Makes** 24

- 1 ripe medium banana
- ¼ cup nut butter
- 12 ounces dairy-free bittersweet chocolate
  Flaky sea salt, for sprinkling

1. Line 2 mini muffin pans with foil liners. In a small bowl, mash banana with nut butter; set aside.
2. In a small bowl, microwave chocolate in 20-second intervals, stirring in between, until melted and smooth.
3. Drop a scant teaspoon of chocolate into each liner, then spoon 1 teaspoon nut-butter mixture on top. Top with about 1 teaspoon chocolate, spreading to cover. Sprinkle each with sea salt and freeze until firm.

Peppermint Trees

Heat oven to 350°F. Coat the insides of metal tree cookie cutters with **nonstick cooking spray** and place them on a parchment-lined baking sheet. Arrange green **peppermint candies** (breaking them as necessary) inside the cutters; there should be space between the candies. Bake until candies melt, 5 to 6 minutes. Let cool completely, then gently pop out.

TRIM THE TREE

After baking, let candies cool 1 minute, then, with a greased skewer, make a small hole in each candy. Let cool completely, then gently pop out of molds and string with ribbon.

Chewy Chocolate-Walnut Cookies

Active Time 10 minutes | **Total Time** 30 minutes | **Makes** 15

Nonstick cooking spray, for the pan

3 cups confectioners' sugar

¾ cup Dutch process cocoa powder

½ teaspoon kosher salt

2 large eggs, at room temperature

1 teaspoon pure vanilla extract

1 cup toasted walnuts, chopped

½ cup bittersweet or dark chocolate chips

Flaky sea salt

1. Heat oven to 350°F. Line 2 baking sheets with parchment paper and lightly coat with cooking spray.

2. In a medium bowl, whisk together sugar, cocoa powder and salt; set aside.

3. Using an electric mixer, mix together eggs and vanilla in a large bowl. Add sugar mixture and mix to combine; fold in walnuts and chocolate chips.

4. Spoon mounds of dough (about 1 ½ tablespoons per cookie) onto the prepared sheets, spacing them 2 inches apart, and sprinkle with flaky sea salt.

5. Bake, rotating the positions of the baking sheets once, until cookies are puffed and tops begin to crack, 12 to 14 minutes. Let cool on baking sheets for 5 minutes, then slide parchment (and cookies) onto a wire rack to cool completely.

GET TOASTY

For that ideal cookie crunch, here's how to toast nuts perfectly: Heat oven to 350°F. Place whole nuts in a single layer on a rimmed baking sheet. Bake, stirring occasionally, until nuts just begin to brown. Immediately transfer to a plate to cool.

How to Master Gluten-Free Baking

1

Store gluten-free ingredients separately to avoid cross-contamination.

2

Whisk together gluten-free ingredients for extra aeration and lift.

3

Avoid overbeating eggs. It can make them more difficult to mix into dough and affects the structure of the finished treat.

4

Prevent gluten-free dough from sticking to the pans by lining them with parchment paper.

STICKY SWEET

This beloved Brazilian party staple is a cross between a fudgy truffle and chewy caramel. Lightly butter or wet your hands before rolling to keep the sweet chocolatey delicacy from sticking to your palms.

Brigadeiros

Active Time 30 minutes
Total Time 30 minutes, plus chilling
Makes 18 to 22

1	14-ounce can sweetened condensed milk
¼	cup unsweetened cocoa powder
2	tablespoons unsalted butter
1	tablespoon espresso powder
⅛	teaspoon kosher salt
¼	cup chocolate sprinkles
¼	cup mixed red and green sprinkles
¼	cup roasted shelled pistachios, finely chopped

1. In a medium saucepan, combine condensed milk, cocoa powder, butter, espresso powder and salt. Whisking often, bring to a boil and wait until mixture melts completely. Reduce heat to medium-low and cook, stirring constantly with a silicone spatula and scraping the sides and bottom of the pan, until mixture pulls away from the sides of pan and forms a thick mass, 4 to 5 minutes more.

2. Spread cocoa mixture on a large plate and refrigerate 30 minutes. Line a baking sheet with parchment paper. Using a tablespoon-size cookie scoop, gently drop mounds onto the prepared baking sheet. Freeze 20 minutes.

3. In 3 separate shallow bowls, place chocolate sprinkles, red and green sprinkles and pistachios. Roll cocoa mounds into balls, then coat some with sprinkles and remaining balls with pistachios. Place in mini candy liners and refrigerate in an airtight container for up to 1 week.

Chocolate-Dipped Coffee Meringues

Active Time 25 minutes | **Total Time** 1 hour 10 minutes | **Makes** 96

¼ cup sugar

1 tablespoon instant espresso powder

⅛ teaspoon cream of tartar

2 large egg whites

4 ounces bittersweet chocolate, coarsely chopped

1. Heat oven to 200°F. Line 2 baking sheets with parchment paper.

2. In a large metal or glass bowl, whisk together sugar, espresso powder and cream of tartar; whisk in egg whites. Set the bowl over (but not in) a saucepan of simmering water; cook, whisking constantly, until sugar is dissolved and whites are very warm to the touch, 2 to 3 minutes.

3. Remove from heat and, using an electric mixer, beat on low speed, gradually increasing the speed to high, until soft, glossy peaks form, about 5 minutes.

4. Spoon egg white mixture into a pastry bag fitted with a 3/4-inch star tip. Pipe stars (about 1-inch wide) onto the prepared baking sheets and bake until meringues are just set on the outside, 25 to 30 minutes.

5. Slide the sheets of parchment paper onto wire racks and let cool completely. Slide a spatula underneath meringues to release.

6. In a small bowl, microwave chocolate in 20-second intervals, stirring in between, until melted and smooth. Dip the tops of meringues into melted chocolate, letting any excess drip off, then transfer to the parchment to let set, about 20 minutes.

STEADY SURFACE

To keep the paper from shifting when you're piping the meringues, place a small dab of the egg white mixture on the corners of the baking sheet, then lay the parchment paper on top.

NO-BAKE BONBONS

Place these peanut butter classics, also known as buckeyes, into matching mini cupcake liners for gifting.

Peanut Butter Balls

Active Time 30 minutes
Total Time 55 minutes
Makes 32

- 2 cups confectioners' sugar
- 1 cup creamy peanut butter
- 4 tablespoons unsalted butter, at room temperature
- 1 teaspoon pure vanilla extract
- ¼ teaspoon kosher salt
- 9 ounces bittersweet chocolate, chopped

Flaky sea salt and melted red candy melts, for decorating

1. Using an electric mixer, beat sugar, peanut butter, butter, vanilla and salt in a large bowl on medium speed until dough forms into a ball, about 2 minutes.

2. Line 2 baking sheets with parchment paper. Roll dough into 1-inch balls and place onto one of the prepared sheets. Freeze until firm, about 20 minutes.

3. Once balls are firm, place chocolate in a small measuring cup and microwave in 30-second increments, stirring between each, until melted and smooth.

4. Working with a fourth of the balls at a time (keep remaining frozen), dip into chocolate one at a time, letting excess drip off, and then place onto the other prepared sheet. Sprinkle with flaky salt if desired. Repeat with remaining peanut butter balls.

5. Once chocolate has set, decorate with melted red candy melts if desired. Keep refrigerated until ready to serve.

Candy Cane Meringues

Active Time 30 minutes **Total Time** 1 hour 45 minutes, plus cooling **Makes** 48

4 large egg whites

½ cup sugar

¼ teaspoon cream of tartar

¼ teaspoon pure peppermint extract

Red and silver gel food coloring

SWITCH IT UP

For a colorful twist, try these with green food coloring, or experiment with different flavored extracts like almond or orange.

1. Heat oven to 200°F. Line 2 baking sheets with parchment paper.

2. In a large metal or glass bowl, whisk together egg whites, sugar and cream of tartar. Set bowl over (but not in) a saucepan of simmering water and cook, whisking constantly, until sugar has dissolved and whites are very warm to the touch, 3 to 4 minutes.

3. Remove from heat and, using an electric mixer, beat on low speed, gradually increasing speed to high, until glossy soft peaks form, about 5 minutes. Beat in peppermint.

4. Fit a pastry bag with a ½-inch round pastry tip. Using a paintbrush, paint vertical stripes of food coloring inside the pastry bag. Spoon egg white mixture into the bag and pipe 1-inch circles onto the prepared baking sheets.

5. Bake meringues until just set on outside, 60 to 75 minutes. Transfer to a wire rack to cool completely.

Reindeer Chow

Active Time 20 minutes **Total Time** 20 minutes **Makes** 12 cups

9	cups Rice Chex cereal
1	cup semisweet chocolate chips
½	cup creamy almond butter
4	tablespoons unsalted butter
½	teaspoon kosher salt
½	teaspoon pure vanilla extract
2	cups confectioners' sugar, divided
1½	cups red candy-coated chocolates (we used M&M's)

1. Place cereal in a large bowl and set aside. In a separate large bowl, microwave chocolate chips, almond butter and butter in 15-second intervals, stirring in between, until melted and smooth. Stir in salt and vanilla. Pour mixture over cereal and gently fold until well coated.

2. In a resealable gallon-size bag, combine half of cereal mixture and half of sugar. Seal, then shake until cereal is evenly coated. Transfer to a bowl.

3. In the same bag, repeat with remaining cereal and sugar. Transfer to the same bowl and fold in candy-coated chocolates. Store at room temperature in an airtight container for up to 1 week.

Coconut Chocolate Truffles

Active time 25 minutes **Total time** 1 hour 20 minutes **Makes** 30

**20 ounces dairy-free dark chocolate
(72% cacao or higher), very finely chopped**

¾ **cup unsweetened coconut milk (well stirred)**

Toasted coconut flakes, for decorating

1. Place half of chocolate in a medium bowl. Heat coconut milk until hot to the touch, then pour over chocolate. Cover bowl loosely with a towel and let stand 5 minutes, then stir until melted and smooth.

2. Chill bowl until chocolate is firm enough to scoop but not rock hard, about 30 minutes. Scoop and roll tablespoon-size balls onto 1 piece of parchment paper; refrigerate.

3. Meanwhile, in a medium bowl, microwave remaining chocolate in 20-second intervals, stirring in between, until melted and smooth.

4. Working 1 at a time, dip balls in chocolate, tapping off excess. Before chocolate has set, sprinkle with toasted coconut flakes if desired.

RECIPE INDEX

HEARST
HOME

Copyright © 2024 by Hearst Magazine Media, Inc.
All rights reserved. The written instructions in this volume
are intended for the personal use of the reader and may be
reproduced for that purpose only. Any other use, especially
commercial use, is forbidden under law without the written
permission of the copyright holder.

Cover and book design by Mariana Tuma
Text by Drew Salvatore
Library of Congress Cataloging-in-Publication Data is available
10 9 8 7 6 5 4 3 2 1

Published by Hearst Home, an imprint of Hearst Home Books/
Hearst Communications, Inc.
300 West 57th Street, New York, NY 10019

Good Housekeeping, Hearst Home, the Hearst Home logo,
and Hearst Home Books are registered trademarks of Hearst
Communications, Inc.

For information about custom editions, special sales, premium
and corporate purchases: hearst.com/magazines/hearst-books

Printed in China
978-1-958395-66-0

PHOTO CREDITS

Mike Garten: Front Cover, 3, 5, 6, 8, 9, 11, 13, 15, 16, 18, 19, 21, 25,
26, 27, 28, 31, 33, 34, 35, 37, 39, 41, 45, 48, 49, 50, 53, 54, 55, 56, 58,
59, 61, 62, 63, 64, 65, 68, 69, 71, 73, 74, 76, 78, 79, 80, 81, 83, 85, 87,
89, 93, 97, 99, 101, 103, 104, 105, 106, 109, 114, 116, 117, 119, 120, 121,
122, 123, 128, 129, 131, 133, 135, 136, 137; Back Cover; Becky Luigart-
Stayner: 23, 43, 118, 130; Brian Woodcock: 12, 75; Burcu Avsar: 110;
Con Poulos: 42, 95, 100; Colin Faulkner: 115; Danielle Daly: 13; Erik
Bernstein: 93; Frances Janisch: 32; Getty Images: 127; Jonny Val-
iant: 88; Jose Picayo: 47; Kat Teutsch: 113; Kate Sears: 22, 44, 67;
Lisa Hubbard: 134; Marcus Nilsson: 29, 66, 91, 92, 93. Ren Fuller:
98; Sarah Anne Ward: 57, 124, 126, 132; Steve Giralt: 38, 84, 111, 112.